Deerfield Public Library
920 Waukegan Road
Deerfield, IL 60015

DEERFIELD PUBLIC LIBRARY

P9-BYO-547

Praise for *Student Loan Solution*

"*Student Loan Solution* is a must-read for aspiring Financial Grownups. The book is specific and practical—perfect for busy people who want solutions, not homework. David Carlson outlines a simple five-step process for understanding student loans and making the best plan possible. Carlson also hits on emergency funds, mental health, money mindset, and much more. You will wish you had read this book sooner."

—Bobbi Rebell CFP®, host of the *Financial Grownup* podcast and author of *How to be a Financial Grownup, Proven Advice from High Achievers on How to Live Your Dreams and Have Financial Freedom*

"*Student Loan Solution* is the go-to book for borrowers who need straightforward and actionable advice on how to deal with their student loan debt. *Student Loan Solution* provides all the information a borrower needs to know about their student loans, in a format that is jam packed with easy to follow tips and advice. The book also provides valuable strategies on how to improve your finances within the context of student loans, something other personal finance books fall short of."

—Shannah Compton Game CFP®, MBA, host of *Millennial Money* podcast

Deerfield Public Library
920 Waukegan Road
Deerfield, IL 60015

WITHDRAWN

"As young Americans face rising tuition costs and over $1.5 trillion in existing college debt, *Student Loan Solution* couldn't be hitting shelves at a more pivotal time. Throughout his book, Carlson utilizes personal experience and an objective, numbers-based approach to cover the gamut of student loans and repayment options. In a concise yet detailed format, you'll learn how to successfully tackle your student loans and lay the foundation for a bright financial future in the process. I am thrilled to recommend *Student Loan Solution* to the diverse range of students I work with nationwide."

—Tara Falcone, CFA, CFP®, Founder of ReisUP and creator of collegiate financial literacy program, LIT™

"An exceptionally well written and informative book on everything you need to know about student loans. David Carlson's first-hand account with student loan debt makes this book relatable and inspirational. *Student Loan Solution* delivers where other books fail to address the impact on finances, relationships, and mental health. David's writing exudes passion and knowledge to help anyone struggling with student loans regain control of their finances beyond debt repayment into a living a better life. *Student Loan Solution* is a must-read for those struggling with student loans or anyone thinking about getting student loans."

—Jason Vitug, author of *You Only Live Once: The Roadmap to Financial Wellness and a Purposeful Life*

Student Loan Solution

Also By David Carlson:

Hustle Away Debt

Student Loan Solution

5 Steps to Take Control of Your Student Loans and Financial Life

David Carlson

Mango Publishing
CORAL GABLES

Copyright © 2019 David Carlson.
Published by Mango Publishing Group, a division of Mango Media Inc.

Cover and Layout Design: Roberto Núñez

Mango is an active supporter of authors' rights to free speech and artistic expression in their books. The purpose of copyright is to encourage authors to produce exceptional works that enrich our culture and our open society.

Uploading or distributing photos, scans or any content from this book without prior permission is theft of the author's intellectual property. Please honor the author's work as you would your own. Thank you in advance for respecting our author's rights.

For permission requests, please contact the publisher at:
Mango Publishing Group
2850 S Douglas Road, 2nd Floor
Coral Gables, FL 33134 USA
info@mango.bz

For special orders, quantity sales, course adoptions and corporate sales, please email the publisher at sales@mango.bz. For trade and wholesale sales, please contact Ingram Publisher Services at customer.service@ingramcontent.com or +1.800.509.4887.

Student Loan Solution: 5 Steps to Take Control of Your Student Loans and Financial Life

Library of Congress Cataloging-in-Publication number: 2018957864
ISBN: (print) 978-1-63353-898-6, (ebook) 978-1-63353-899-3
BISAC category code STU031000, STUDY AIDS / Financial Aid

Printed in the United States of America

Disclaimer:

This book is for informational purposes only and may or may not apply to your specific situation. Please do your due diligence and consult with an accountant, tax professional, certified financial planner, and/or other professionals for advice on your specific situation before making decisions that impact your finances.

The author has made every effort to give accurate and timely information, but rules, laws, and processes referenced are subject to change and accuracy cannot be guaranteed.

This book is dedicated to anyone who has ever struggled with student loans.

Table of Contents

Foreword

Being in student loan debt can make you do crazy things.
Things you never thought possible—like moving back in with
your mother.

At twenty-three, I dismantled my tidy, IKEA-trimmed
apartment, sold some of my belongings, put the rest in boxes,
and moved back into my childhood bedroom, with tape from my
old Jonathan Taylor Thomas posters still stuck to the walls. My
mother informed me my curfew would be eleven and dating was
highly discouraged.

"Mom, I'm in my mid-twenties," I said.

"Pfft," she replied. "I don't care if you're *thirty*."

She may have been strict, but my mom taught me the value of
money at an early age. When I was eight, I stuffed dollar bills
into my piggy bank to save up for toys and books. My mom
would say, "every little bit counts," and she was speaking from
experience. When she was in her mid-twenties, my mom worked
full-time in the cheese department at Kroger and part-time at
Sunny's, a convenience store down the street from our tiny,
one-bedroom apartment. Somehow, on that meager income, my
mom saved ten thousand dollars. She packed up her own one-
bedroom apartment and moved us to a safer part of town. She
wanted better for me: a better education, a better job, a better
financial life.

Maybe that's why I hated being in student debt so much. I was
the first in our family to go to college, and, at twenty-three, I was
earning twenty-five thousand dollars a year. It wasn't much, but,
for a family that spent most of the time struggling financially,
this was kind of a big deal. There was so much I wanted to buy
with that salary—a trip to Europe after college or a brand-new
wardrobe—but I had a student loan to repay, and I couldn't
ignore it. Being in debt is like driving around with a weird,

clunky car noise. You can try to pretend it's not there, but you know better. Ignoring it will only make it worse.

Fueled by that frustration, I was determined to get out of debt. I didn't just move back in with my mom; I took on part-time babysitting jobs. I had a side hustle selling used cowboy boots on eBay, like a less stylish Sophia Amoruso. After a year or so, I paid off my twelve-thousand-dollar student loan.

This may be the part where you scoff. After all, twelve thousand dollars is nothing compared to today's average student loan borrower, who carries a debt of nearly forty thousand dollars. Back then, my student loan seemed insurmountable on my meager salary, so I can't imagine being thrust into the workforce, smack-dab in the middle of a crisis. Hundreds of news articles and headlines dissect who is to blame for this student loan crisis. (I've written some of these articles, and the gist of it is: more students, less funding, and shady lenders and education-based businesses.) In truth, there are a number of entities to blame, which makes it easier for each of them to shirk responsibility and pass it onto the borrower, who dared try to afford to get a college education in the first place. The consequences reverberate through our economy nonetheless.

Headlines would have you believe Millennials are to blame for all our economic woes. We're not buying homes, we're not getting married—these headlines imply Millennials have a choice in the matter, as if we have $200,000 on hand for a down payment, but we're postponing homeownership because we're such darn procrastinators. The reality is Millennials are postponing homeownership for the same reason I'm postponing getting a star on the Hollywood Walk of Fame: it's just a tad unrealistic.

We have little control over the economy, but we do have choices. We can choose to learn how the system works and become advocates for its repair by voting at the polls and voting with our dollars. We can also learn personal finance—the options we have for managing our own money and getting rid of our own debt.

For this reason, I'm grateful that this book and Carlson's previous one, *Hustle Away Debt*, exist. I won't pretend the solutions outlined here are as easy as moving back into your childhood bedroom. If you're reading this, however, you probably already know how much of a struggle it is to be in debt. Like me, you're probably also hell-bent on climbing out of it, which is why you're reading this book in the first place.

On the pages that follow, Carlson explains your options for getting rid of your student debt—options many people don't even know exist. You'll learn how to organize your finances. How to pick a repayment strategy. You'll even learn how to manage your own mental health as you're going through the whole process, which will at times feel grueling, but is 100 percent worth it.

Amid all of this practical help, Carlson does the seemingly impossible. He gives us hope, something we need now more than ever. Wages have barely moved since the Great Recession, the income gap continues to widen, and student loan debt continues to soar. When it comes to money, hope doesn't come easy. The good news is, you're in the right place. Now more than ever, you need this book.

—KRISTIN WONG

Author, *Get Money: Live the Life You Want, Not Just the Life You Can Afford*

Drowning in Student Loans

$100,000.

As in one hundred THOUSAND dollars! This number will always
a hold a special place in my heart.

Why, you may ask? Perhaps it's the amount I was paid to write
this book? Ah. No. It is how much my wife and I had in student
loan debt when we graduated from college.

It translated into approximately one thousand dollars a month in
loan payments.

One thousand dollars a month. At the time, we were paying a
similar amount on rent. Think about what we could have done
with an extra thousand dollars a month!

One thousand dollars a month for a newly married couple. I
was working as a staff accountant and my wife was a psychology
major with dreams of getting her PhD. She was between
undergrad and grad school, working a couple of part-time jobs as
she studied for the GRE.

My wife needed to at least obtain a master's degree to do
the work she had been dreaming of and working toward in
undergrad. I was planning on getting an MBA, so I could leverage
it to get a better job with higher pay, be more competitive in
the marketplace, and learn new skills. But adding the cost of
two master's degrees seemed a little less attractive when we
were staring one hundred thousand dollars of undergrad debt
in the face.

I played out scenarios in my head. Would an MBA even make
sense? Did I even want to stay in corporate America forever? If I
ever wanted to leave my corporate job to run a business, was that
even an option with so much student loan debt? I struggled with
this decision for years, but, in the short term, I moved on to more
pressing matters: our monthly student loan payments.

Faced with our debt, my wife and I did a number of things to improve our finances, many of which we will go over in this book. One thing in particular was the creation of a side income stream. It was my student loans that gave me the motivation to start my blog *Young Adult Money* in 2012. I wanted the blog, and other side income streams, to bring in enough money to cover the thousand dollars of cash flow we were losing each month to student loan payments. One thousand dollars a month was the *minimum* monthly payment on the standard ten-year repayment plan. Unless we put more toward our loans, we would be making those payments year after year for ten full years.

The blog led to my first book, *Hustle Away Debt*, which was a comprehensive overview of side hustles, including what to do before starting one, how to pick the right one for you, and how to optimize and grow your side hustle. Side hustles dominated my life. I was always looking for new ways to make extra money or grow and scale my existing income streams.

The focus I put on side hustles was directly due to my student loan debt. Everything points back to that one-hundred-thousand-dollar mountain of debt welcoming me to "the real world." It was a source of stress and anxiety. Short- and long-term money decisions were made in the context of it. It may have motivated me to stick with my side hustles, but I also felt like I *had* to focus on them. Updating our student loan balances wasn't typically a cause for celebration, because it didn't feel like the balances were going down that quickly.

Too often I've read blogs, articles, and books aimed at those in their twenties and thirties that fail to recognize that student loans are at the center of financial decisions for those who have them. "Just cut your expenses and pay off your loans faster" is something you may have heard. This advice is rarely caveated with the fact that, for some borrowers, student loans are such a big expense that even cutting expenses by 25 percent won't prevent them from living from paycheck to paycheck. Nor does the advice typically mention a more helpful first step, analyzing whether an income-driven repayment plan can help a borrower gain financial stability, free up cash flow, and avoid falling behind on loans.

That's why I wrote this book. It's long past time for a book on student loans that is comprehensive yet simple, blunt but empathetic. A book that leaves you feeling in control and confident. Hopeful for the future. Ready to take action. A book that tells you to go after your dreams and goals, to live the life you deserve, and to no longer have student loans constantly weighing you down.

If you're reading this, either you or someone close to you has student loans. I know this because over forty million people have student loans in the United States.

Across those forty million-plus borrowers, there is over one and a half trillion dollars in outstanding debt.[1] Roughly 70 percent of students graduate from college with student loans, and the average amount of student loan debt for a borrower in the class of 2017 was more than thirty-seven thousand dollars.[2]

You may have more or less than the average borrower. Deferment, forbearance, or falling behind and defaulting may have caused your balance to increase significantly. You may feel resignation when you think of your loans. Tired, perhaps.

---

1   *The Federal Reserve,* https://www.federalreserve.gov/releases/g19/HIST/cc_hist_
    memo_levels.html. Q2 2018.
2   Mitchell, Josh. "Student Debt Is About to Set Another Record, But the Picture Isn't All
    Bad," *The Wall Street Journal,* https://blogs.wsj.com/economics/2016/05/02/student-
    debt-is-about-to-set-another-record-but-the-picture-isnt-all-bad/. May 2016.

On an uplifting note, there are repayment plans that may help
you move to a more affordable monthly payment. There may
even be potential opportunities to have your loans forgiven
after ten, twenty, or twenty-five years of repayment. I will be
the first to admit that, in the past, I was ignorant of the variety
of repayment and forgiveness options, as well as the details
surrounding each. It's complicated. There's a reason that one
million new borrowers default on their loans every year[3] and why
you may have been one of them.

Until you pay them off, student loans stick with you. They linger.
It feels like you have no recourse. You can't simply declare
bankruptcy and have them disappear. In fact, you defaulting
on your loans is actually *profitable* for the government and
loan servicers because it leaves you with a higher loan balance.
Student loan debt is a unique sort of debt; it's not normal.

And can we talk a minute about the reams of unhelpful advice,
and uninformed and unempathetic opinions, that people share
about student loans?

"You should have gone to community college first...You
should have chosen a different university...You should have
worked more."

Should have. Could have. Would have.

Unhelpful. Unnecessary. And usually, unsolicited.

Or how about comments like "I'm so glad I didn't have to take
out loans. That would be terrible! I don't know what I would do."

---

3   Based on data from the *National Student Loan Data System*, https://catalog.data.gov/
     dataset/national-student-loan-data-system. August 2018.

I'll just say what you are probably thinking when you hear this: we can't all withdraw free college from the Bank of Mom and Dad.

This book is written for those who have already taken on college debt. It's important not to dwell on things you can't change. Student loans are one of those things. Your energy needs to be spent on looking ahead, not back.

Student loans can take a mental toll on borrowers. This can result in negative thoughts and an unhelpful, if not damaging, mindset. Because of that, instead of diving into the process of understanding your loans, I want to start by talking about your money mindset.

Student Loans and Your Money Mindset

Money mindset could very well be a new concept to you. It encompasses the beliefs, attitudes, and emotions that come to mind when we are dealing with money-related issues.

Whether you like it or not, your money mindset has been shaped inadvertently by how you were raised and the situations that you are in currently and have been through in the past.

For example, whoever raised you may have displayed an attitude of limitation when it comes to money. They may have made comments about there "never being enough money" and conveyed a feeling of helplessness in regard to increasing their income or generally improving their financial situation. If you grew up with a parental figure expressing this mindset, you may either mimic their mindset or go in the other direction, where you do anything in your power to make more money and push your finances forward.

If you currently have student loans, you may have feelings of hopelessness and resignation, especially if you've had them for years and have seen your balance barely decrease or even increase. You may have been unable to move forward with anticipated life milestones like buying a home, saving for retirement, or even moving out of your parents' basement. Similar to how your upbringing impacts your money mindset, your student loan situation also influences your views and beliefs about money.

Money mindset is important because our finances touch every area of our lives and affect our long-term trajectory. If your money mindset is one of limitation, where you think things like "I will have student loans forever," you aren't going to be motivated to leave no stone unturned in your quest to pay down and exert control over your student loans. Leanna Haakons, founder of financial marketing firm Black Hawk Financial and author of *Young, Fun & Financially Free*, stresses the impact that positive mindset can have on your life: "By being in the right money mindset, you know where you're headed, what your priorities and goals are, and how you're going to get there. No matter where you're coming from, you need to try as much as possible to stay positive and focused on your end goals and lifestyle values. Know what you're working for and where you're headed, no matter where you're starting from."

Haakons recognizes that student loan debt is one of those big challenges that can create a negative mindset. She says, "Of course, if you have a big obstacle in front of you from the outset, rather than a clean slate, it is going to be a challenge to keep your mindset strong." Being self-aware about your mindset, especially around money, is important. Most people don't regularly practice being aware of their thoughts or how their thoughts impact their energy and mood (for better or worse). Without actively focusing on a positive money mindset, it's easy to slip into unproductive or even destructive thoughts that will prevent you from sticking with a big goal, such as mastering your student loan debt. For many it can even lead to complete inaction, a sort of personal purgatory.

Having a positive mindset and outlook starts with you—not with your partner, not with your friends, not with your family. And this positive mindset absolutely can translate into taking actions that, over both the short and long term, will improve your life. Haakons adds, "If you have the access, you have the option. For example, within the book you're reading right now," (Yup, this one.) "you have access to a wealth of information about student loans and improving your financial life. Because you have access to this information, you have the option, and the ability, to change your current and future life."

This all builds to the following key point:

You do not have to delay your happiness until your loans are gone.

This is the theme that underlies this entire book. My desire for you is that you will put in the time and energy necessary to gain control over your student loans, take the necessary actions to put your finances on a positive course, and live a life of happiness, regardless of the amount of debt you have. It may take some time, or even a long time, to pay down your student loans, but that doesn't mean you can't be happy *now*.

You may be cynical about the power of positive thinking and changing your mindset, but it could be the difference between moving forward to a more positive financial situation and being stuck where you are at.

Many negative things that we tell ourselves or that others tell us about money are straight-up lies. And student loans can certainly cause us to repeat these lies. You may be burned out and beaten down from your student loans and finances. You may have trouble envisioning a "better" life or even one where your debt isn't soul-crushing.

"I don't deserve better."

"I will never make enough money."

"I will always be behind where I should be financially."

"My life will never be what I want it to be."

"My loans make me a burden."

"I am stupid for taking out student loans."

These are all lies. Perhaps it's just you telling yourself this, but it could be others speaking these lies into your life. If anyone in your life is speaking these lies to you, you need to seriously consider whether they deserve to be in your life.

Here are some truths to speak into your life:

"My self-worth has nothing to do with my net worth."

"Through discipline and commitment, I can eliminate my debt and put myself in a better place financially."

"My dream life is possible."

"I am valued."

Seek out people who are on your side, who encourage you, and who want to see you succeed. And remember, it all starts with your mindset. You can do this!

Throughout this book, there will be a number of action items. While you can do most action items within the book, I recommend downloading the free companion guide at StudentLoanSolutionBook. com. This website has a number of companion materials you can download and utilize while reading *Student Loan Solution*:

- PDF Companion Guide

- Student Loan Spreadsheet

- Budget Spreadsheet (two versions to choose from) and Budget Printables

What lies do you tell yourself, or have you been told, about your student loans, your money, and your life? List them.

_____

_____

_____

_____

_____

_____

_____

Now list truths about your student loans, your money, and your life. For example, if a lie you wrote down was "I am a drag on others because of my student loans," write "My self-worth has nothing to do with my net worth. I have value."

Don't be afraid to get specific here, and try to include examples from
your life when possible.

_____

_____

_____

_____

_____

_____

_____

_____

Keep these truths close to you, either on a note card or a sticky note
on your desktop.

Say them out loud, and even shout them out! You are capable of
doing great things!

- -

Let's shift our focus to creating a student loan plan and strategy.
Too often we hear a one-size-fits-all solution. These "solutions"
do not take into consideration your unique situation, such as
what loans you have, what your income is, what your repayment
options are, whether you have an emergency fund, and so forth.

*I want you to find a solution to your
student loans that works for you.*

Let's look at a hypothetical situation. If you have a low income and are in a career that you want to stay in, there are options for you to make your student loans more manageable. That may mean moving into an income-driven repayment plan, starting a side hustle, or making sacrifices elsewhere. But, at the end of the day, you need a plan of action that works for your specific situation. It may not be realistic for you to double your income or cut 50 percent of your expenses which may be the only way you could pay off your loans on the standard ten-year repayment plan (more on that soon).

Some finance gurus will tell you that you should hate your student loans so much that you can't stand the thought of them. While some have responded well to this message, I am in favor of a more balanced approach to paying off student loan debt which allows you to:

- Build an emergency fund.
- Pay off high-interest debt.
- Invest for retirement.
- Use repayment options that align to your situation.

It's worth noting that there is nothing wrong with going "all out" and depriving yourself until your loans are gone. It's one option, but not the *only* option.

As you go through the process of creating and implementing your student loan strategy, including identifying and making smart money moves that improve your situation, you will quickly realize that not everyone will end up with the same student loan strategy. And that's a good thing! Your situation is unique to you, and your strategy should reflect that.

A Step-by-Step Plan to Gain Control

The goal of the five-step process in this book can be summed up in one word: control.

You can have control over your student loans, and your greater financial life, by gaining knowledge and understanding about them and combining that with the various aspects of your unique financial situation. This empowers you to take the necessary actions with confidence that you are pushing forward in the right direction.

It's not fair, but you need to spend more time managing your money than those without student loans. If you're willing to put in the time and effort, you can craft a student loan strategy that fits your unique situation. Creating and implementing this strategy will give you the freedom to pursue the life that you may otherwise feel is out of reach.

We'll go step by step through a five-step system that will leave you with a solid plan and strategy for your student loans, as well as strategies you can use on a regular basis to continue to improve your financial life.

Step 1: The Starting Point—Know Your Loans

In step one, you will gather all your student loan information and put together a student loan snapshot. This snapshot will include necessary information for your student loan strategy. You will also learn about the different types of student loans, including consolidation loans, and the differences between them.

Step 2: The Possibilities—Understand Your Options

In step two, you will learn about your repayment options, opportunities for loan forgiveness, and tools such as refinancing, forbearance, and deferment. Having a full understanding of the options available to you is critical for feeling in control of your loans and confident in the choices you make. Student loan default is also covered, including how to get out of it and back on track.

Step 3: Your Money—Understand Your Financial Situation

Knowing the ins and outs of your student loans and repayment options isn't enough to make an effective student loan plan. You also need to understand your financial situation. Things like how much cash flow you have, how much of an emergency fund you have (if you have one at all), what debt you have besides student loans, and other considerations are all important factors in determining your repayment strategy.

Step 4: Decision Time—Choose Your Repayment Strategy

At this point, you will have full knowledge of your student loans, repayment options, and your financial situation. In this step, you combine all this information and choose the best repayment strategy for you.

Step 5: A Brighter Tomorrow—Optimize Your Money

Having a repayment strategy is great, but don't stop there. Your situation today doesn't have to be your situation tomorrow. I'll share strategies and hacks that will allow you to continually improve your situation and put yourself in a better financial spot.

In addition to these five steps to a successful student loan plan, we'll dive into a few specific areas that student loans tend to impact.

Bonus Section: Your Student Loans and Your Life

Mental health and relationships are two areas where student loans can have a big impact. Additionally, student loans pose a problem for people who go to school for a career and then realize it's not the right fit for them. We will talk about all of these things in this section.

Whether you've spent no time looking into your student loans or have spent some time getting familiar with them, going through this five-step process will provide you the knowledge necessary to gain control of your situation and give you confidence to know that you are moving in the right direction.

Step 1:

The Starting Point–
Know Your Loans

When I think back to when I took out my college loans, I don't remember much. My parents filed my FAFSA for me. They chose the loans they thought I should take out. I was grateful I didn't have to deal with it and went along with whatever they proposed.

I mean, the decision was made that I was going to college, right? I couldn't control how much or how little my parents contributed toward my college education. I didn't set tuition at the college of my choice. I never considered switching schools based on how much tuition was or what financial aid package I would receive. I chose the "best" college I got into, the one that "felt right" after the campus visit. The cost of college, and how much debt I would leave with, was an afterthought.

My parents may have explained the difference between subsidized and unsubsidized federal loans, but I never cared enough to truly understand. And even if I did understand the details at the time, I certainly didn't retain this information. I didn't keep a running tally of my loans. I didn't review them regularly or see the impact of interest while I was in deferment.

While you may have been more hands-on with your student loans, I would bet a majority of borrowers relied on their parents or another authority figure to take care of their loan applications and decisions. It's very common for graduates to not know what types of loans they have or how much they owe.

The reality is that when high school seniors are picking a college, they are making an emotional—not financial—decision.

Once a college is chosen, students typically do not switch for financial reasons. If their financial aid package, including loans, can cover the cost, students tend not to think about the impact loans will have when they graduate. Many have likely thought at one time or another, "Everyone takes out loans, so I should too." Debt quickly becomes an afterthought.

It's also not uncommon for those who have been out of school for a while, even years, to be a bit clueless about their student loan debt. They may have put it in forbearance or fallen behind on their loans and gone into default.

Understanding your loans is the first step to having control over your loans and your financial life.

The type of student loan(s) you have matters. It impacts:

- Repayment options, including eligibility for income-driven repayment plans
- Opportunities for loan forgiveness
- How interest is treated when loans are in deferment or forbearance

First, we'll create a snapshot of your loans by finding all your loan information and putting it in a spreadsheet. This spreadsheet will be an important reference for the rest of the book.

Your Student Loan Snapshot

Creating your student loan plan starts with knowing what
student loans you have. Thankfully, gathering this information is
relatively straightforward if you know where to look.

> One last word of advice before you do this: **brace yourself.**
>
> If you haven't gone through this exercise before, what you
> see may not be pretty. Your debt may be tens of thousands of
> dollars higher than expected. This initial step could very well
> be the most difficult—but necessary—step in gaining control of
> your loans.

If you are shocked at the number you see after you total up your
debt, take some deep breaths. You are going to get through this.
It may not be easy, but ignorance is *not* bliss. Knowing your
situation and taking action is key.

For federal student loans, go to the National Student Loan Data
System website at https://www.nslds.ed.gov/nslds. You will need
to create a Federal Student Aid identification number (FSA ID) if
you don't already have one.[4]

Once you are logged in, you can see your loans. Clicking on each
loan will give you additional information, including the loan
servicer, the interest rate, and the history of your loan, including
when it went into repayment.

You may also have private loans. If you are unsure which bank or
banks serviced your loans, you will want to find out. The best way

---

4   While not required, you may have already created an FSA ID to sign your FAFSA or to
    access your data online.

to do this is to pull your free credit report at AnnualCreditReport. com. Your credit reports will include all your student loans, regardless of whether they are private, federal, or state. Once you identify the lender, get access to their online portal to see detailed information about your loans.

State loans will be on your credit report as well. These are much less common than federal loans, but they do exist. Both my wife and I took out student loans offered by the state of Minnesota to fund our undergrad education.

Even if you are aware of all your loans, it's always a good idea to pull your credit report from the three credit reporting bureaus, especially if it's been more than a year since you last pulled it or if you have never done so. You are entitled to a free credit report from each bureau once a year. See a useful overview of credit starting on page 215.

Gather all your student loan information and put it into the student loan spreadsheet found here: StudentLoanSolutionBook.com.

Key information to find out includes:

- **Type of Loan**
  If you have federal loans, note whether they are from the Federal Direct Loan Program (FDLP) or Federal Family Education Loan (FFEL) Program, as well as whether they are subsidized or unsubsidized. This will be indicated when you log in and click on your loan information. It's okay if this doesn't mean anything to you right now—it will soon!

- **Loan Servicer**
  There are a limited number of loan servicers for federal
  student loans. They include companies like Navient,
  Nelnet, and MOHELA. It's not uncommon to have a
  variety of servicers for your loans.

- **Principal Amount**
  The amount of money that you currently owe on
  your loans.

- **Accrued Interest**
  Interest accrues in certain situations on certain loans,
  such as when your loans are in forbearance or deferment.
  Interest can also accrue if you are in an income-driven
  repayment plan and your monthly payment doesn't cover
  all the monthly interest.

- **Revised Principal Amount (Principal plus
  Accrued Interest)**
  In most cases, the accrued interest is eventually added
  to the principal of a loan through a process called
  capitalization. Looking at your principal balance plus
  accrued interest gives you a look at the true balance of your
  student loans.

- **Interest Rate**
  The percentage of the principal charged as interest by
  the lender.

- **Fixed or Variable Interest**
  Federal student loans have a fixed interest rate, but others,
  such as private loans, can have a variable interest rate that
  fluctuates over time.

- **Monthly Payment (If Known—This Can Be
  Calculated)**
  You may have a good idea of what your monthly payment
  is, especially if you have already started to pay your loans

on a standard ten-year repayment plan. You can get an estimate of your monthly payment under that standard plan in one of the tabs of the student loan spreadsheet[5] by plugging in your loan variables (principal, interest rate, etc.). If it seems high or unaffordable, don't panic. For federal student loans, there are income-driven repayment plans available, which we will cover in step two. If you only have private student loans and your payment is unaffordable, we'll cover that in step two as well.

- **Projected End Date (Estimate)**
  Assuming you are on the standard ten-year repayment plan, this can usually be calculated relatively easily. If you are on an income-driven repayment plan, this will be more difficult to calculate. This date isn't necessary, but, in some situations, it can be helpful.

As you read about the various types of loans, you can refer back to your spreadsheet to determine which types you have.

The Different Types of Student Loans

Not all loans are created equal. As you likely saw on your student loan snapshot, there are a variety of loan types.

Generally speaking, student loans can be put into three buckets: federal, private, and state. Federal loans are the most common. Private and state loans are less common, though private loans have been increasing in popularity recently.

---

5   This is within the same spreadsheet you are adding your student loan info to, which is available for download here: StudentLoanSolutionBook.com.

Going through the different types of loans may be overwhelming, but gaining this knowledge is important for the ultimate goal of feeling in control of your loans.

Federal Student Loans

There are two federal student loan programs: the William D. Ford Federal Direct Loan Program (FDLP) and the Federal Family Education Loan (FFEL) Program.

The FFEL program will only impact you if you took out college loans prior to the 2008–2009 school year (I did). It's been discontinued since 2008.

The FFEL program was only slightly different from the William D. Ford Federal Direct Loan Program. Loans in the FFEL program originated at private institutions, meaning these private institutions funded the loans. The federal government paid fees to the private institutions to originate and administer the loans. Eliminating the FFEL eliminated the private institutions that were middlemen in the process. This contrasts with the FDLP, where the government raises funds through debt offerings.

The Department of Education administers loans through the FDLP via the Office of Federal Student Aid. These loans are approved through the Department of Education and disbursed by the borrower's school. Once disbursed, the loans are assigned to a loan servicer (Nelnet, Navient, etc.). The loan servicer is responsible not only for collecting on the loans, but also for communicating information to borrowers while they are in school and when they enter repayment.

Federal student loans come with benefits that you won't find with private student loans. Interest rates on federal student loans are fixed and are usually relatively low.[6] Borrowers have options to consolidate their loans, as well as delay payment on their loans through deferment and forbearance. They also have the ability to enter into income-driven repayment plans and potentially have their loans forgiven.

Not counting consolidation loans, which combine a variety of different types of loans, these are the different loan types offered through FDLP and FFEL:

Federal Direct Loan Program

- Direct Loan Subsidized Stafford

- Direct Loan Unsubsidized Stafford

- Direct Loan Unsubsidized Stafford—Graduate or Professional Students

- Direct Loan PLUS—Graduate or Professional Students

- Direct Loan PLUS—Parent

Federal Family Education Loan Program

- FFEL Subsidized Stafford

- FFEL Unsubsidized Stafford

- FFEL Unsubsidized Stafford—Graduate or Professional Students

- FFEL PLUS—Graduate or Professional Students

- FFEL PLUS—Parent

One of the most important concepts related to federal student loans is the difference between subsidized and unsubsidized loans. Subsidized loans are preferable, especially if you plan on

---

6   Some private student loans do have low, fixed interest rates, but this typically is only the case when you refinance (see page 54).

going to grad school, in which case most people put their loans in deferment.

Direct subsidized loans start accruing interest only when you start repaying your loans. Meaning, interest is not building on these loans while you are in undergrad or grad school, nor when you defer your loans. Note that interest *does* accrue if you enter forbearance (more on that in a bit).

Direct unsubsidized loans are less advantageous than federal direct subsidized loans because interest starts accruing as soon as the loan is disbursed. If you were disbursed an unsubsidized loan as a freshman, for example, you started accruing interest immediately.

Once you enter repayment, typically six months after finishing undergrad, all your accrued interest is added to the principal balance of your loans through a process called capitalization. This pushes up the overall amount you must repay. You then pay interest on that new, higher principal amount. Ditto for grad school.

With unsubsidized loans, the interest is going to continue to build and ultimately be added to the principal of your loan through capitalization. This happens regardless of the reason for deferment. Not surprisingly, unsubsidized loans can accrue considerable interest while you are in grad school, whereas subsidized loans accrue nothing.

One thing to keep in mind is that, if your loans are in deferment, you can continue to make payments toward them. If possible, it's typically a good idea for grad students to continue to make payments toward their loans, at least enough to cover the interest on their debt. Doing this will prevent your accrued interest from building while you complete your grad degree. Some people can take years to finish their master's or PhD, and, if no payments are made, the balance will continue to grow on unsubsidized loans.

Direct subsidized loans are only available for undergraduate students. Once you enter grad school, you either have to take out unsubsidized loans or PLUS loans, which we will go over next.

Direct PLUS Loans

Direct PLUS loans are available to graduate students, as well as parents of dependent undergraduate or graduate students. Similar to unsubsidized direct federal student loans, the interest starts accruing as soon as the loan is disbursed.

We will go over income-driven repayment in step two; however, it's worth mentioning that if you consolidate your loans and the consolidation loan pays off a Parent PLUS loan, your repayment options are more limited when it comes to income-driven repayment than if you had left that loan out of the consolidation. If you've already done this, no worries—I will lay out your options. If you haven't done it yet, I would advise proceeding with caution if you are looking into consolidation.

Direct Consolidation Loans

Consolidation is just what it sounds like: combining multiple loans into one loan. Contrary to popular belief, consolidating your loans will not save you money or make your interest rate "cheaper." All the loans being consolidated are weighted, so the final interest rate and monthly payment that gets set for your loan will be just as "expensive" as what you were previously paying for all your loans.

If you are curious or considering consolidating, you can see what your weighted interest rate is by using the tool on one of the tabs within the student loan spreadsheet. If you haven't downloaded it yet, you can get it here: StudentLoanSolutionBook.com.

Consolidation is different from refinancing. Refinancing your student loans through a private lender *can* save you money by giving you a lower interest rate, but you also no longer have a federal loan and give up all your rights to income-driven repayment and the potential for forgiveness.

Consolidation may make sense for you for a number of reasons:

- **Simplicity**—You may have ten or more student loans, and they may be spread out among various loan servicers. Consolidation combines your loans into one loan that will have one servicer.

- **Variable to Fixed Interest**—Your new consolidation loan will have a fixed interest rate, which can be ideal if interest rates continue to rise.

- **If You Have a FFEL Loan**—Direct loans are the only loans eligible for most of the income-driven repayment plans. If you have an old FFEL loan, you can, in essence, turn it into a direct loan, because any consolidation loan created today *is* a direct loan.

  You can also include Federal Perkins loans in a Direct Consolidation Loan, but it does come with drawbacks. Federal Perkins loans that are included in a Direct Consolidation Loan are bucketed under the "unsubsidized" portion of the loan. That means interest accrues during times of deferment. Normally, Perkins loans do not accrue interest during deferment.

- **To Exit a Grace Period Early**—The six-month grace period following graduation is a mandatory grace period that cannot be waived. Why would you want to get out of a grace period early? For one, if you are working toward Public Service Loan Forgiveness and want to start making progress toward your 120 required payments, you need to be out of the grace period and in an income-driven repayment plan. Consolidating your loans gives you the option to forgo the remainder of your grace period and start making payments immediately.

- **To Make Defaulted Loans Current**—Loan consolidation is one of the ways a borrower can make their defaulted student loans current.[7]

Drawbacks of a consolidation loan include:

- If you are on an income-driven repayment plan and working toward loan forgiveness, either through Public Service Loan Forgiveness or the standard forgiveness route, by consolidating, you are creating a new loan. That means any payments made on the old, now nonexistent, loans would not count toward forgiveness. The clock resets and the timeline starts over.

- When you keep loans separate, you can focus on paying off those with the highest interest rates first. If you consolidate, you have one loan with one interest rate, so you can't strategically pay off individual loans.

---

7   You can find out more about student loan default, including how to exit default, starting on page 62.

- There is no "undoing" a loan consolidation. Similar to refinancing your student loans through a private lender, loan consolidation cannot be undone.

- You generally can only consolidate your loans once.

- If you consolidate a Parent PLUS loan, your new consolidation loan is only eligible for one income-driven repayment plan: Income-Contingent Repayment (ICR). While this is better than having no income-driven repayment option, it's best to keep any Parent PLUS loan out of a consolidation loan, so that you can potentially have other income-driven repayment options.

Because of the complexities around consolidation loans and student loans in general, I recommend you hold off applying for loan consolidation until you feel comfortable with all your repayment options and fully understand how loan consolidation would impact your options.

If you do want to consolidate your student loans, you can do so at studentloans.gov.[8]

Perkins Loans

Perkins loans are made through the Federal Perkins Loan Program. They are much less common than FDLP and FFEL loans, but they do exist, and you may have them. They differ from FDLP and FFEL loans in that Perkins loans are issued by your school. In other words, your school is the lender.

Some schools do not participate in the Federal Perkins Loan Program, so for some borrowers they were never even an option.

These loans have a low interest rate of 5 percent. They are available to undergraduate, graduate, and professional

---

8   Full URL: https://studentloans.gov/myDirectLoan/launchConsolidation.action

students. They are only available to those with "exceptional financial need."

Private Student Loans

Based on data collected by the College Board, we know that, over the past eight years, the number of private student loans has increased.[9]

There are a number of factors driving the recent uptick. The cost of college has increased, forcing more undergrads to supplement federal student loans with private student loans. Additionally, the student loan refinancing market has seen explosive growth, with more and more banks offering student loan refinancing products.

Private student loans are not inherently a bad option, but they do have disadvantages compared to federal student loans. Federal loans typically offer lower interest rates, with some private student loans reaching 10 percent and beyond. This can potentially be adjusted to a lower interest rate through refinancing down the road, but there are restrictions that banks put on the refinancing products that make it difficult or impossible to refinance while in school and without, at a minimum, a good credit score.[10]

Many of the advantages that federal student loans provide are not offered for private student loans. For example:

- Income-driven repayment is not an option.

- Loan forgiveness is not offered.

---

9   "Trends in Student Aid," *The College Board*, https://trends.collegeboard.org/student-aid/figures-tables/total-federal-and-nonfederal-loans-over-time

10   A good credit score is 650 or higher. You can read more about credit and credit scores starting on page 215.

- When in deferment, federal subsidized loans do not accrue interest, but private student loans do accrue interest (similarly to unsubsidized federal loans).

- Private student loans technically are in default as soon as you are behind on payments, while federal student loans go into default much later (after nine or more months of non-payment).

When you are prioritizing which loans to repay first, it makes sense to put private student loans at the top of the list. Even if you have federal student loans that you are paying on an income-driven repayment plan, you will want to pay as much as you can toward your private student loans. With no option for loan forgiveness, you will eventually need to pay them off.

Refinancing private student loans at a lower interest rate through a private lender usually makes sense. Refinancing federal student loans is a potential misstep, as you would lose all the benefits that come with federal loans. We'll discuss refinancing in detail in step two. It may or may not make sense for your situation.

State Student Loans

Some states offer student loans to state residents who are attending an eligible school.

I went to college in my home state, Minnesota, and was able to take advantage of their SELF loan program, which is administered by the Minnesota Office of Higher Education. These loans bear a lower interest rate than federal loans.

Besides sometimes having a lower interest rate, state student loans typically are not on par with federal student loans. For example, here are some details of the Minnesota SELF loan, per their website:[11]

- You need to pay interest every three months while you are in school, starting within ninety days from when you receive the money.

- You must start repaying certain SELF V loans no later than nine years from when you received the money.

- There are no grace periods or deferment options.

- SELF loans cannot be included in a federal loan consolidation.

And here are the two SELF loan repayment options for when you finish your studies (unless you are already in a required repayment period):

- The Standard Plan requires monthly payment of principal and interest starting thirteen months after you leave school or start attending less than half-time.

- The Extended Interest Plan allows you to continue with two more years of monthly interest payments before starting to repay the amount (principal) you borrowed.

These loans are better than private student loans, but they do have their disadvantages, such as not having interest deferment or a forbearance option.

I shared details of this program with you because you may have some loans from a state program yourself. If you do, be sure to read all the documentation available online. If you still have questions or are unclear on anything, reach out to the loan servicer or administrator of the program. It's important to know

---

11   *Minnesota Office of Higher Education,* https://www.selfloan.state.mn.us/
faq.cfm. Q2 2018.

what rights you have, what the terms are, and what happens to
the loans if you enter grad school.

Key Takeaways

- People often have loans spread across different loan
  servicers and may have a mix of federal, private, and state
  student loans. Create a student loan snapshot by putting
  the details of your student loans into a spreadsheet.

- Federal student loans are the best type of student loans
  because of the benefits that come with them such as
  deferment, forbearance, income-driven repayment
  options, and loan forgiveness opportunities.

- Subsidized loans are better than unsubsidized
  loans because interest does not accrue during times
  of deferment.

- In most cases, accrued interest eventually gets added to the
  principal of your loan through the process of capitalization.

- Consolidating your student loans can be beneficial but
  should be done with caution and only when you feel you
  fully understand the implications of consolidation.

Step 2:

The Possibilities–
Understand
Your Options

"How am I going to pay back all these loans?"

"I could be paying this the rest of my life!"

"I can't afford these monthly payments."

"Why me? Why couldn't my parents have paid my tuition?"

Have you ever had one of these thoughts? Many people feel distraught or even hopeless when they see how much they owe in student loans, especially when they see what their loans translate to for a monthly minimum payment.

While there is no magic pill to make your loans go away overnight (unless you win the lottery), I've found that many borrowers lack knowledge about their repayment options. This lack of knowledge causes people to feel like they have no control over their situation and is a driver behind the large number of borrowers who default on their loans. After all, if you can't afford the minimum payment, how can you be expected to make it month after month?

In this step, I will lay out your repayment options and how they relate to the types of loans you have. My goal is for you to have the key facts, pros and cons, and implications of each type of repayment plan. Additionally, we will go over things like refinance, forbearance, and deferment, and the implications of taking advantage of them.

Private Student Loan Repayment Options

While my wife was in grad school, we received what seemed like monthly mailers from a couple of banks that tried to get us to take out private student loans to supplement her federal loans. While we did not need to take advantage of these private loans, we did have private student loans from our undergrad years.

Having private student loans is becoming more common, whereas, not too long ago, banks had little on their balance sheets in terms of student loans. Now it seems like every bank wants to get in on them. And why not? Tuition continues to rise, and the amount of outstanding debt has rapidly increased over the past decade.

There is big money to be made in student loan refinancing. Banks are able to pick and choose which borrowers they refinance, and typically those with a solid credit history are the ones who get approved.

There's a lot happening in this space, so let's start by talking through private student loans that you either took out while in school or obtained through refinancing. Then we'll discuss why refinancing is popular and how it may benefit you.

Repaying Private Student Loans

If you have private student loans, you either received them while you were in school or obtained them through refinancing. Either way, this debt differs from federal student loans in a variety of ways.

- **Repayment Terms:** Repayment varies by lender. More likely than not, the standard ten-year repayment plan will be used, but it is possible to get extended repayment (as with everything, depending on the terms the lender offers). Another reason why refinance is popular is that you can pick and choose your repayment terms, as well as choose a fixed or variable interest rate. Some may even argue it's easier to refinance (assuming you have the credit history that makes you eligible) than to work with your current lender.

- **Interest Rate:** Interest rates are typically variable on private loans, while federal loans are fixed. It's not uncommon for a private student loan to have interest rates in the double digits (this is why refinancing at a lower interest rate is becoming more common).

- **Forbearance and Deferment**: Federal student loans offer forbearance and deferment options; private student loans will vary in their offerings. Some lenders may offer neither, while others may offer some variation.

- **Hardship:** If you are unable to make the monthly minimum payment on your private student loans, how the situation is dealt with will vary by lender. Some may offer "interest only" payments for a certain amount of time. Others may offer temporary forbearance.

- **Forgiveness:** It's safe to assume there are no forgiveness options for private student loans. If your payment is too high, it may make sense to focus on staying current on your payments, build a good credit history, and refinance for a longer period of time. One way or another, the lender is going to pursue repayment.

When we walk through the federal repayment options, you'll see that, despite the complexity and variety of repayment options, the rules are uniform. With private lenders, the rules are not uniform and can vary from lender to lender.

Whether you have some private student loans or have refinanced so all your student loans are private, I highly recommend spending some time contacting your lender to figure out what options are available to you.

You can use the questionnaire below as a starting point. You may already know the answers to some of these but, if you are unsure, do not be afraid to ask. You can't have control over your loans if you don't understand them!

Questions to ask your lender:

- What repayment plan am I on? Are there other repayment plans available to me?
- What is my interest rate? Is it fixed or variable?
- Is it possible to switch to a fixed interest rate? What is the process?
- Does my loan offer any sort of forbearance or deferment? If so, what are the details?
- If I lose my job or income and can't make payments, what happens? *Note: this should be explained in the answer to the previous question, but phrasing the question in explicit terms can be helpful if your lender's answer isn't clear.*
- Is there a prepayment penalty if I pay off my loans early?

Getting the basic information around your private student loans is a key first step. You may be happy about what you find out, or your repayment terms and options may leave a lot to be desired.

Find out what the terms of your private loans are, as well as whether there are alternative payment plans.

The good news is that there is little risk in refinancing private student loans. We'll go over that next.

Refinancing Student Loans

If you have student loans, you likely have been inundated with offers (I have) from private companies that want you to refinance your student loans. They promise lower interest rates and potentially thousands of dollars in savings.

When you're in debt and someone offers to save you thousands of dollars, you listen.

Let's use Rebekah as an example. Below are some of the details of her situation:

> Loan Balance: $40,000
>
> Type of Loans: Federal
>
> Interest Rate (weighted average): 8.0 percent

Given these details, on a standard ten-year repayment plan, she will pay $485 a month. If she stays with this plan, she will pay approximately $18,200 in interest over the course of ten years.

If she refinanced all $40,000 of her loans at an interest rate of 6.0 percent, her monthly loans would drop to $444. After ten years she would pay approximately $13,290 in interest. **That's a savings of $4,947, or 27 percent**.

To lock in a lower interest rate and save nearly $5,000 on interest, Rebekah may be willing to give up her rights to forbearance, deferment, income-driven repayment, and loan forgiveness.

Let's take this a step further. If Rebekah was willing to sacrifice and pay $750 a month toward her refinanced loans instead of $444, she could pay them off in approximately five years instead of ten and pay just $6,640 toward interest. **That's an**

additional $6,650 in savings on interest for a total of $11,597, or 64 percent, on interest.

If she didn't refinance to 6.0 percent and stuck with an 8.0 percent average interest rate but still made the higher payments, she would pay off her loans in approximately five and a half years and would still save significantly on interest, approximately $8,600, or 47 percent.

Interest Rate	Principal Amount	Monthly Payment	Repayment Time	Interest Paid	Principal + Interest
8.0%	$ 40,000	$ 485	10 Years	$ 18,237	$ 58,237
6.0%	$ 40,000	$ 444	10 Years	$ 13,290	$ 53,290
8.0%	$ 40,000	$ 750	5 Years, 7 Months	$ 9,594	$ 49,594
6.0%	$ 40,000	$ 750	5 Years, 1 Month	$ 6,640	$ 46,640

One thing to note is that if Rebekah stuck with the ten-year minimum monthly payment plan after refinancing to 6.0 percent and did not contribute anything beyond the required minimum monthly payment, she would still be paying approximately $41 less a month. $41 a month may not seem like much, but that translates to nearly $500 in savings a year. If she were to invest that in a retirement account, she would benefit from her investments gaining value, as well as potentially lower her taxable income (if the retirement account was a 401(k) or standard Individual Retirement Account (IRA)).

Interest rates matter!

This example illustrates exactly why refinancing has become so popular. The banks benefit because they can take the lower interest rate and still profit on other products they sell, while

the borrower benefits because they can save hundreds or even
thousands of dollars on interest payments.

Refinancing private student loans is becoming a no-brainer
for those with good credit. As long as the new lender offers
similar benefits to your current lender in terms of deferment,
forbearance, hardship, and other factors, it usually makes sense
to refinance to a lower interest rate.

With federal student loans, it becomes a more difficult decision.
When you refinance with a private lender, you are eliminating
your current federal student loans. The new lender is paying
them off and, in turn, creating a new loan that is 100 percent
private. That means the following benefits that come with federal
student loans are gone:

- **Opportunities for loan forgiveness:** Public Service
  Loan Forgiveness (PSLF) and other forms of loan
  forgiveness are no longer available to you.

- **Forbearance and deferment:** You will no longer
  have the standard rights to forbearance and deferment
  that come with federal student loans. Make sure you
  understand how the new lender treats hardship situations
  such as a loss of income.

- **Income-driven repayment:** Income-driven repayment
  options help make otherwise unaffordable student loans
  affordable. They cap your payment at 10–20 percent of
  your discretionary income. These are only available for
  federal loans.

For some borrowers, refinancing may still make sense. For
example, if you run the numbers and project you can reasonably
pay off your student loans in three to five years without
stretching your budget too far, you may want to refinance if it
means saving thousands of dollars on interest.

At a minimum, I would encourage people to build a healthy emergency fund, eliminate credit card debt, and factor in retirement savings before they refinance federal student loans. Until these actions have been taken, it's best to keep the protections of federal student loans in place.

Again, refinancing can't hurt if you have private student loans, but proceed with caution if you have federal loans. You can always refinance later if it makes sense, but you cannot "undo" refinancing and go back to your federal loans.

This book spends a significant amount of time covering things like loan forgiveness and income-driven repayment, and I think those topics arc important. But there are still many borrowers out there who will stick with the standard ten-year repayment plan and may benefit from aggressively paying off their student loans. Refinancing could be a part of their plan.

I am all for saving money on student loans through refinancing, but only if you fully understand what you are giving up by doing so.

Forbearance and Deferment

Before we look at federal student loan repayment options, it would be beneficial to spend some time going over deferment and forbearance in more detail. I've mentioned forbearance and deferment a few times already, and you are probably wondering what they are and how they work.

Deferment

In some situations, you are able to temporarily stop making payments on your loans by putting them in deferment. In fact, there's a good chance you've taken advantage of at least one type of deferment (in-school).

Some common scenarios where you can apply for deferment are:

- **In-school**—You can take advantage of in-school deferment when you are enrolled at least half-time at an eligible college or career school, including graduate school. If you are a college grad, you almost certainly took advantage of in-school deferment while you were finishing your degree.

- **Unemployment**—You can defer your loans for up to three years during times of unemployment or when you are unable to find full-time employment.

- **Economic Hardship**—You can defer your loans for up to twelve months at a time during periods of economic hardship or while serving in the Peace Corps for a maximum of three years.

There are additional opportunities for deferment, such as when you are in an approved graduate fellowship program or when you are on active-duty military service in connection with a war, military operation, or national emergency.

Interest While in Deferment

Deferment is one reason subsidized federal student loans are the best type of student loans. While you are in deferment, interest typically will not accrue for this type of loan. Unsubsidized loans, on the other hand, will accrue interest and capitalize once you exit deferment or a grace period following deferment, such as when you graduate or are no longer enrolled at least half-time.

> **Capitalization** is the process of accrued interest being added to the principal balance of your loans.

As most grad students learn, the interest on unsubsidized loans can add up. If you are in grad school for three years or longer, there may be a sizable amount of interest that will be capitalized once you finish. The total accrued can be a bit shocking, particularly if you have a lot of unsubsidized loans and haven't been regularly reviewing your loans (which I would bet is the majority of students).

While deferring student loans during undergrad and grad school usually makes sense, ideally you would continue to make payments that cover the interest on your unsubsidized loans. This will prevent interest from accruing during deferment, which ultimately increases the amount owed. With that said, I know making these payments while in grad school is not realistic for many.

For more information on deferment, to access the forms necessary to request the various types of deferment, or to see additional deferment opportunities, you can visit studentaid. ed.gov.[12] You can also reach out to your loan servicer for more information on how to defer your loans.

---

12   Full URL: https://studentaid.ed.gov/sa/repay-loans/deferment-forbearance#deferment-eligibility

Forbearance

Forbearance is a period of time during which your payments are temporarily suspended or reduced for up to twelve months, at which point you need to reapply. It's a less desirable option than deferment because interest continues to accrue on *all* loans, regardless of what type of loan they are. Once your loans exit forbearance, the accrued interest is added to the principal balance of your loans through capitalization.

With that in mind, deferment is always better than forbearance. And, to be blunt, forbearance should be avoided at all costs.

To illustrate this example, let's say you have forty-five thousand dollars in federal student loans at a weighted average interest rate of 6.5 percent. Below you can see the impact interest will have on your loans, based on how many months you remain in forbearance:

Months in Forbearance	Monthly Interest		Total Accrued		Original Principal		Principal after Capitalization	
1	$	244	$	244	$	45,000	$	45,244
6	$	244	$	1,463	$	45,000	$	46,463
12	$	244	$	2,925	$	45,000	$	47,925
24	$	244	$	5,850	$	45,000	$	50,850

Even if just a portion of your loans were subsidized, you would be better off in deferment. On the flip side, if these were all unsubsidized loans, it wouldn't make a difference whether they were in deferment or forbearance; both would accrue interest that eventually would be added to your principal balance.

There are two types of forbearance: general and mandatory.

General forbearance is at the discretion of your borrower. General forbearances are granted for any reason that is acceptable to the loan servicer. Typical reasons include financial difficulties, unemployment, change in employment, and medical expenses.

There is no supporting documentation required for general forbearance, and you can have it granted through a simple phone call attesting to your reason(s) for needing to put your loans in forbearance. There is no formal limit on how much time you can spend in forbearance, as long as it does not exceed thirty-six months at a time.

Mandatory forbearance must be granted if you meet eligibility requirements. Supporting documentation is required. Circumstances that make you eligible for mandatory forbearance include:

- You are serving in a medical or dental internship or residency program.

- The total amount owed each month for all your student loans is 20 percent or more of your total monthly gross income.[13]

- You are serving in AmeriCorps (in a position where you received a national service award).

- You would qualify for Teacher Loan Forgiveness based on the teaching service you are providing.

- You would qualify for partial repayment of your loans under the US Department of Defense Student Loan Repayment Program.

---

13 In this case, you should move into an income-driven repayment plan instead of applying for forbearance.

- You are a member of the National Guard, have been activated, and are not eligible for a military deferment.

If you have received mandatory forbearance based on your financial situation (i.e. owing 20 percent or more of your total gross income), your ability to continue in it is typically capped at three years.

With all this in mind, should you apply for forbearance? It's almost never an ideal option but, if you are behind on your student loans, applying for forbearance makes your loans current, meaning you will no longer be behind on your payments. This option should be taken only if you are ineligible for deferment and unable to make the payments necessary to cover your missed payments. Additionally, if you are facing economic hardship or unemployment, you should always look to deferment first. With that said, it's better to temporarily enter forbearance than to fall behind on your payments and risk defaulting.

Forbearance should be viewed as a short-term option and only be used when absolutely necessary. To find out more about forbearance and how to apply, visit studentaid.ed.gov.[14]

Student Loan Default

Student loan default is a real problem today. According to a January 2018 report by the Brookings Institution, nearly 40 percent of student loan borrowers may default on their student loans by 2023.[15]

---

14   Full URL: https://studentaid.ed.gov/sa/repay-loans/deferment-forbearance#deferment-eligibility

15   Scott-Clayton, Judith. "The looming student loan default crisis is worse than we thought," The Brookings Institute, https://www.brookings.edu/research/the-looming-student-loan-default-crisis-is-worse-than-we-thought/. January 2018.

For most federal student loans, you will default if you don't make a payment in more than 270 days. What follows isn't pretty. You lose eligibility to receive Federal Student Aid and, even worse, you can face consequences like wage garnishment or tax refund withholding.

The general steps in default are:[16]

1.   You haven't made a payment for more than 270 days.[17]

2.   The entire balance, both principal and interest, becomes immediately due.

3.   You lose access to options like deferment, forbearance, and repayment plans.

4.   You either make repayment arrangements with the holder of your loan, or your loan gets placed with a collection agency.

5.   The collection agency will offer the option of a voluntary repayment agreement.

6.   If you don't enter into the voluntary repayment agreement, or fail to make the agreed payments, the collection agency will take actions such as wage garnishment. If you are self-employed and they cannot garnish your wages through an employer, the US Department of Justice may take legal action—by suing you—to collect on the defaulted loans.

Unfortunately, around a million borrowers default on their student loans each year, and even more are behind on payments at one time or another.[18] You may be behind on your payments

---

16   Derived from this page on studentaid.gov: https://studentaid.ed.gov/sa/repay-loans/default/collections

17   This usually doesn't actually happen until 360 days, as lenders have 90 days to file a default claim and most wait until the end of the claim period.

18   Based on data from the *National Student Loan Data System*, https://catalog.data.gov/dataset/national-student-loan-data-system. August 2018.

or in default yourself. Let's go through a couple of scenarios and see what options are available to you.

Scenario 1: If You Are behind on Payments but Haven't Defaulted

If you are behind on payments on your student loans but have not yet defaulted, you need to get out of delinquency ASAP, so you don't default.

The simplest, though perhaps most unrealistic, way to get your student loans current is to make up the missed payments. For most who have missed payments, this will only be realistic if you are only two or three months behind. The other, more common, approach is to apply for deferment or forbearance.

If you are granted deferment or forbearance by your loan servicer and you have any missed payments, your loans will be made current. In plain terms, if you are current on student loans, you are no longer behind on payments. Deferment is preferable to forbearance, due to the potential for the government to pay some or all of your interest depending on the type(s) of loans you have. Deferment is also more difficult to obtain than forbearance.

If you have multiple student loan servicers, you need to work with each separately to enter deferment or forbearance. It's important to reach out to your loan servicers as quickly as possible if you are behind on your student loans, as they can help you get out of delinquency before you reach the more harmful stage of default.

Scenario 2: If You Defaulted on Your Student Loans

If your student loans are in default, there are a couple of options to get out of default and make your loan(s) current.

Option #1: Loan Rehabilitation

Loan rehabilitation is one way to get out of default. Loan rehabilitation starts with contacting your loan holder. Rehabilitation doesn't immediately make your loans current. Instead, you must first make nine payments during a period of ten consecutive months.

The payments are determined by you and your loan holder. These payments are deemed "reasonable" based on your financial situation. How this is determined is by taking 15 percent of your annual discretionary income and dividing by twelve. Discretionary income is your income above and beyond 150 percent of the federal poverty level. We'll go through the calculation in more detail shortly (see page 73). You must provide documentation to your loan holder for the amount to be calculated.

In rehabilitation, the minimum payment is five dollars a month. The reason is that the lender wants to make sure you get in the habit of voluntarily making monthly payments, even if the amount is as low as five dollars.

Once you have made the nine agreed-upon payments, your loan will no longer be in default. You will no longer be subject to wage garnishment and you will be eligible for deferment and forbearance. Your access to student aid will be restored and you will be eligible for loan forgiveness programs.

Once your loans are current, you will want to get on an income-driven repayment plan to ensure that your payments going forward are affordable. The whole ordeal likely will make you realize how serious defaulting is and how important it is to stay on top of your loans.

Note that fees of up to 16 percent of the value of your loans may be charged for loan rehabilitation. While I understand there are costs that go into all the different actions the government takes for loan rehabilitation, I still think this is kicking you while you are down. If you think about why someone would default on their student loans, it likely was due to not having full information or knowledge around options like deferment, forbearance, and income-driven repayment. Their payments were likely unaffordable for their financial situation, so tacking on a 16 percent charge seems unreasonable to me and doesn't set someone up for success in repayment. Nevertheless, let's move on to option number two, loan consolidation.

Option #2: Loan Consolidation

The other option for getting out of default is loan consolidation. Consolidating your loans allows you to quickly make your defaulted loans current. There are no required payments you have to make.

Loan consolidation, like loan rehabilitation, can include fees being added to the balance of your student loans. In the case of loan consolidation, you could see fees of up to 18.5 percent. It could also be worse for your credit score, since the record of the defaulted loans will stay on your credit history for seven years. This is not the case with loan rehabilitation.

With loan consolidation, you must enter an income-driven repayment plan unless you make three voluntary, on-time, full monthly payments on the defaulted loans *prior* to consolidation. These payments will be determined by your loan holder but must be reasonable and affordable for your financial situation. If you make these payments, you will be able to choose any repayment plan available.

Delinquent Student Loans and Your Credit Score

Just as being late or missing credit card payments can hurt your credit score, missing payments on your student loans can wreak havoc on it.

Your payment history accounts for 35 percent of your total credit score. This has a bigger impact on your credit score than how much you owe, the length of your credit history, or any other factor. Making regular, timely payments on your debt is important for a healthy credit score but, by the time you default on your student loans, you have at least nine full months of missed payments.

It's also worth noting that exiting default through loan consolidation does not remove the record of default from your credit history. You will have to wait a full seven years for that to happen. Loan rehabilitation does remove the record of default from your credit history, but the late payments that happened before your loan went into default will stay on your credit history for seven years.

Because of the impact that being delinquent and defaulting on your student loans can have on your finances, I highly recommend that student loan borrowers look into income-driven repayment plans, deferment, forbearance, and in general understand the options available to them that would help avoid default. If you can't afford your loans, there are options available.

Federal Student Loan Repayment Options

When borrowers enter repayment on their federal student loans, they are automatically put in a standard ten-year repayment plan. This happens regardless of whether a borrower's income can accommodate the payments.

Many stay on this standard plan until their loans are paid off. But others fall behind and potentially default on their loans, which has unfavorable effects on their credit and increases their balance and the projected time it will take to pay back their loans.

The standard ten-year plan isn't the only plan, though. Not everyone realizes this. It takes time and effort to actually learn about and understand the other options, and, even if people know they exist, they may not know whether their loans are eligible.

By the end of this section you will understand the various plans available for federal loans, including the standard ten-year repayment plan, the income-driven repayment plans, and other plans.

Repayment Plans Available for Federal Student Loans:

- Standard Ten-Year
- Income-Driven
- Graduated
- Extended

Standard Ten-Year Repayment

All federal loan servicers are required by law to initially put loans in the standard ten-year repayment plan. This plan features 120 fixed monthly payments. You will pay less interest in the standard ten-year repayment plan than any other plan.

Despite having fixed payments over the life of the loan, the percentage of your payment that goes toward the principal increases over time; conversely, the percentage of your payment that goes toward interest decreases over time. This is due to the fact that interest is accrued daily on the principal of your loan. As that principal goes down, and the payments remain fixed, naturally a greater amount of the fixed payment goes toward the principal.

Let's use Marla as an example. Here are the details of one of her loans:

> Loan Balance: $14,000
>
> Interest Rate: 6.4 percent
>
> Term: 10 years

The fixed monthly payment for this example would come to approximately $157.55. In the first month, the payment would be split 53.35 percent toward the principal and 46.65 percent toward interest.

Here's a visual example of how this works. Note that this example is based on a 360-day calendar for simplicity's sake. The actual split of each payment may be impacted by the day of the month that the payment is processed on and the exact number of days in a given month.

Month	Starting Principal	Payment $	Payment Principal	Payment Interest	% of Pmt Principal	% of Pmt Interest	Remaining Principal
1	$ 14,000	$ 157.55	$ 84.05	$ 73.50	53.35%	46.65%	$ 13,916
12	$ 13,051	$ 157.55	$ 89.03	$ 68.52	56.51%	43.49%	$ 12,962
24	$ 11,951	$ 157.55	$ 94.80	$ 62.74	60.17%	39.83%	$ 11,856
36	$ 10,780	$ 157.55	$ 100.95	$ 56.60	64.08%	35.92%	$ 10,679
48	$ 9,533	$ 157.55	$ 107.50	$ 50.05	68.23%	31.77%	$ 9,426
60	$ 8,205	$ 157.55	$ 114.47	$ 43.08	72.66%	27.34%	$ 8,091
72	$ 6,791	$ 157.55	$ 121.89	$ 35.65	77.37%	22.63%	$ 6,669
84	$ 5,285	$ 157.55	$ 129.80	$ 27.75	82.39%	17.61%	$ 5,156
96	$ 3,682	$ 157.55	$ 138.22	$ 19.33	87.73%	12.27%	$ 3,544
108	$ 1,975	$ 157.55	$ 147.18	$ 10.37	93.42%	6.58%	$ 1,828
120	$ 157	$ 157.55	$ 156.72	$ 0.82	99.48%	0.52%	$ (0)

If you haven't already, you can plug in your loans in the standard ten-year repayment tab of the student loan spreadsheet available at StudentLoanSolutionBook. com to get an idea of how much you are paying toward principal and interest.

Initially it may feel like you aren't making much progress on your loan. In this example, in the first five years of repayment, Marla will pay off approximately six thousand dollars of her principal, compared to the final five years, when she will pay off approximately eight thousand dollars. This is the nature of interest, though, and is also why making extra payments toward the principal lessens the amount of time you are in repayment. As that principal gets lower and lower, the amount going to interest decreases.

Income-Driven Repayment

With a quarter-million new borrowers defaulting on their federal student loans each month,[19] it has never been more important for borrowers to know about income-driven repayment plans.

---

19   Based on data from the *National Student Loan Data System*, https://catalog.data.gov/ dataset/national-student-loan-data-system. August 2018.

Income-driven repayment is becoming much more popular, which is both a good and bad thing. It's a bad thing because it highlights the growth of the student loan problem and how unaffordable college has become. It's a good thing because it potentially helps borrowers avoid default. Some of the specific reasons these plans have become more popular include:

- Opportunity for monthly payments as low as zero dollars. (Yes, you read that right: ZERO dollars.)

- They are eligible for Public Service Loan Forgiveness (PSLF).

- If you aren't eligible for PSLF based on your current employment, you may be able to have your loans forgiven after twenty or twenty-five years of on-time payments under an income-driven repayment plan.

- The average amount of student loans per borrower has increased drastically while wages have stagnated, causing a larger percentage of borrowers to be in a position to benefit from income-driven repayment plans.

- Borrowers are starting to realize these are options for repayment that can help them avoid forbearance and default.

Income-driven repayment plans work exactly as the name suggests: your monthly student loan payment is based on your income. To be specific, your Adjusted Gross Income and family size are factored into the equation. The adjusted payment is capped at 10 to 20 percent of discretionary income.

There are four income-driven repayment plans, as listed below, starting with the most favorable and ending with the least favorable:

- Pay As You Earn (PAYE)

- Revised Pay As You Earn (REPAYE)

- Income-Based Repayment (IBR)

- Income-Contingent Repayment (ICR)

We'll go through the details of each of these plans, but first we'll go over what loans are eligible for each plan, as well as how discretionary income is determined.

What Loans Are Eligible?

Already refinanced your federal student loans through a private lender? Move on to Step 3: Your Money—Understand Your Financial Situation.

Despite your loans not being eligible for income-driven repayment or forgiveness, the good news is that banks are fighting for your business. That means more potential for saving on interest, which can amount to thousands of dollars saved. If you missed it or need to revisit, we talk about refinancing starting on page 54.

The details of each of the four income-driven repayment plans follow, but generally only loans from the Federal Direct Loan Program (FDLP) qualify.

Note: Parent PLUS loans (direct PLUS loans made to parents of dependent undergraduate students) currently do not qualify (on their own) for *any* income-driven repayment plans.

The only way Parent PLUS loans can qualify is if a borrower entered repayment on or after July 1, 2006, and the loan is part of a Federal Direct Consolidation loan. That Direct Consolidation Loan is eligible for the Income-Contingent Repayment (ICR) plan. In general, though, you should avoid including Parent PLUS loans in a loan consolidation as it limits your income-driven repayment plan options to the ICR, which is the least favorable of the four plans.

Private, state, and federal student loans that were refinanced through a private lender *do not* qualify for an income-driven repayment plan. Here is a summary of eligible loans for each plan:

- **PAYE:** All direct loans except Parent PLUS loans and consolidation loans that repaid Parent PLUS loans.

- **REPAYE:** All direct loans except Parent PLUS loans and consolidation loans that repaid Parent PLUS loans.

- **IBR:** All direct loans and FFEL loans except Parent PLUS loans and consolidation loans that repaid Parent PLUS loans.

- **ICR:** All direct loans except Parent PLUS loans. Consolidation loans made after July 1, 2006, that repaid Parent PLUS loans are eligible.

How Is Discretionary Income Determined?

Not surprisingly, discretionary income is the most important variable for income-driven repayment. The higher your discretionary income, the higher a monthly payment the government assumes you can afford; conversely, the lower your income, the lower your monthly payment. If you have no income or a relatively low income, the government may not require you to pay anything.

To determine discretionary income for the purpose of income-driven repayment plans, there are two things we need to determine:

- Your monthly income

- What amount of income can be carved out per the federal poverty guideline.

The calculation is as follows: discretionary income equals gross income minus 150 percent of the poverty guideline.

Let me define each of these in more detail.

Note: For Income-Contingent Repayment (ICR), you factor in 100 percent of the poverty guideline to calculate discretionary income, not 150 percent like the other income-driven repayment plans.

Monthly Income

The monthly income calculation is relatively straightforward. It's the lower of the following:

- Previous tax year's Adjusted Gross Income (AGI) divided by twelve

- Current monthly gross income (before taxes and pre-tax deductions)

More likely than not, your AGI will be what is used for the discretionary income calculation. If you filed taxes last year, your AGI will be shown on your tax filing.

Curious what the "Adjusted" means in Adjusted Gross Income? It may help to look at gross income. Gross income is how much money you make before taxes or deductions are taken out. Once you take out deductions, such as the standard deduction, your AGI is lower than your gross income.

Federal Poverty Guidelines

Each year, the Department of Health and Human Services releases poverty guidelines.[20] To determine the amount you can subtract from your income for the purpose of calculating

---

20   The most recent guidelines can be found here: https://aspe.hhs.gov/poverty-guidelines

discretionary income, you take the federal poverty guideline for your household size and multiply it by 150 percent. The exception is ICR, which takes 100 percent of the federal poverty guideline instead of 150 percent.

There are separate poverty guidelines for the forty-eight contiguous states, Alaska, and Hawaii, as can be seen below for 2018.

These tables feature 2018 data; since things are always changing, you may want to check the most recent guidelines within the student loan spreadsheet on StudentLoanSolutionBook.com.

Federal Poverty Guidelines - 2018

48 Contiguous States and the District of Columbia			
Persons in Family / Household	Poverty Guideline	Poverty Guideline 150%	Monthly 150%
1	$ 12,140	$ 18,210	$ 1,518
2	$ 16,460	$ 24,690	$ 2,058
3	$ 20,780	$ 31,170	$ 2,598
4	$ 25,100	$ 37,650	$ 3,138
5	$ 29,420	$ 44,130	$ 3,678
6	$ 33,740	$ 50,610	$ 4,218
7	$ 38,060	$ 57,090	$ 4,758

Alaska			
Persons in Family / Household	Poverty Guideline	Poverty Guideline 150%	Monthly 150%
1	$ 15,180	$ 22,770	$ 1,898
2	$ 20,580	$ 30,870	$ 2,573
3	$ 25,980	$ 38,970	$ 3,248
4	$ 31,380	$ 47,070	$ 3,923
5	$ 36,780	$ 55,170	$ 4,598
6	$ 42,180	$ 63,270	$ 5,273
7	$ 47,580	$ 71,370	$ 5,948
8	$ 52,980	$ 79,470	$ 6,623

Hawaii			
Persons in Family / Household	Poverty Guideline	Poverty Guideline 150%	Monthly 150%
1	$ 13,960	$ 20,940	$ 1,745
2	$ 18,930	$ 28,395	$ 2,366
3	$ 23,900	$ 35,850	$ 2,988
4	$ 28,870	$ 43,305	$ 3,609
5	$ 33,840	$ 50,760	$ 4,230
6	$ 38,810	$ 58,215	$ 4,851
7	$ 43,780	$ 65,670	$ 5,473
8	$ 48,750	$ 73,125	$ 6,094

Let's go through the details of each of the income-driven repayment plan options, starting with PAYE, which is the most favorable plan for borrowers.

Pay As You Earn (PAYE)

The highlights of Pay As You Earn:

- Student loan payments are generally 10 percent of your discretionary income and never more than you would pay under a standard ten-year repayment plan based on the balance of your loans when you entered PAYE.

- Partial loan forgiveness after 240 qualified payments, or twenty years.

- You must have a partial financial hardship (PFH) in the year you apply.

- Loans from the Federal Direct Loan Program (FDLP) are the only loans that are eligible.

  Reminder: Parent PLUS loans and consolidation loans that repaid Parent PLUS loans are *not eligible*. The only income-driven repayment plan these loans are eligible for is Income-Contingent Repayment (ICR).

- You must have been a new borrower as of October 1, 2007 OR had no prior outstanding loan balances AND taken out a new direct loan on or after October 1, 2011.

- Your spouse's income affects the calculation, unless you file your taxes as *married filing separately*.

Ineligible? You aren't alone, especially if you deferred loans while in grad school. My wife and I are both ineligible for PAYE, as we started undergrad just prior to the cutoff to qualify as a new borrower. Jump to the Revised Pay As You Earn (REPAYE) section, which is the next-best option for borrowers.

PAYE Example

Let's walk through an example of what PAYE looks like.

Robert is single, lives in Missouri, and his previous tax year's AGI was $35,000, or $2,917 a month. His income has not changed significantly since he filed taxes last year.

Based on the poverty guideline for a single person in Missouri, calculated at 150 percent, we get $18,210 for a full year or $1,518 per month.

Robert's monthly discretionary income is:

$2,917−$1,518=$1,399

Under the PAYE plan, payment would be approximately 10 percent of $1,399, or $140.

Let's say Robert has $100,000 in student loan debt, and all of his loans are FDLP loans that qualify for the PAYE repayment plan.

If his monthly payment under the standard ten-year repayment plan is $1,000, he will pay $860 less on a PAYE repayment plan than he would on the standard ten-year repayment plan.

If you are eligible, PAYE is the best income-driven repayment plan.

PAYE gives you the option—but not the requirement—to exclude your spouse's income and debt from the repayment calc. While this does require you to file your taxes as married filing separately, which comes with its own disadvantages, as long as you are in the PAYE plan you at least have the option to do so.[21]

---

21 In some cases, married filing separately *will* make sense, but the pros and cons of this approach are beyond the scope of this book. It can't hurt to talk to a tax accountant about the implications of each approach (filing jointly, married filing separately) for your situation.

Consider Robert's situation. If he were to marry someone who has no student loans and has an AGI of $130,000 a year and they filed their taxes jointly, all the income would be counted in the calculation, pushing the minimum payment up significantly.

Let's assume Robert and his spouse's AGI was a combined $165,000, or $13,750 a month.

Based on the poverty guideline for a two-person household in Missouri, calculated at 150 percent, we get $24,960 for a full year or $2,058 per month.

Robert and his spouse's monthly discretionary income is:

$13,750−$2,058=$11,692

Under the PAYE plan, payment would be approximately 10 percent of $11,692, or $1,170.

Assuming Robert's minimum monthly payment was $1,000 under the standard ten-year repayment plan, he would not have a partial financial hardship, or PFH, and would not qualify for PAYE.

Even if Robert and his partner's AGI was slightly lower and he did qualify for PAYE, his payment would be significantly higher when his spouse's income (and lack of student loan debt) was factored in.

Partial Financial Hardship

Two of the income-driven repayment plans (PAYE and IBR) require you to have a PFH in the year you apply. But what the heck is it?

A PFH exists under these scenarios:

- Your calculated monthly payment under PAYE at 10 percent of your discretionary income is less than the required payment under a standard ten-year fixed repayment plan.

- Your calculated monthly payment under Income-Based Repayment at 15 percent of your discretionary income (or 10 percent for qualified "new borrowers"[22]) is less than the required payment under a standard ten-year fixed repayment plan.

Let's simplify this. Both of these scenarios compare a potential payment under an income-driven repayment plan (either PAYE or IBR) to a payment under the standard ten-year repayment plan.

Let's walk through an example. Here are the details of Charlie's situation:

Balance of all federal loans: $50,000

Weighted Interest Rate: 6.4 percent

Adjusted Gross Income (AGI) from last year's taxes: $40,000

No spouse and no children

Step 1: Monthly payment under the standard ten-year repayment plan

Calculates to $565 using our spreadsheet tool

Step 2: Monthly payment under PAYE

---

22   To be an eligible "new" direct loan borrower for IBR, you must satisfy a couple of requirements: You have not taken out a federal direct loan prior to July 1, 2014, and have no outstanding balance on a FFEL Program loan when you receive a direct loan on or after July 1, 2014.

Adjusted Gross Income-150 percent of the Federal Poverty Guideline=Discretionary Income

$40,000–$18,210=$21,790

Annual Discretionary Income×10 percent/12 Months=Required monthly payment under PAYE

$21,790×10 percent/12=$182

Step 3: Monthly payment under IBR (assume he is not a new borrower)

Adjusted Gross Income-150 percent of the Federal Poverty Guideline=Discretionary Income

$40,000–$18,210=$21,790

Annual Discretionary Income × 10 percent/12 Months=Required monthly payment under PAYE

$21,790×15 percent/12=$272

Step 4: Compare payments

Standard Ten-Year Repayment Plan vs. PAYE: $565 vs. $182

Standard Ten-Year Repayment Plan vs. IBR: $565 vs. $272

Based on these calculations, Charlie has a PFH because his payment under PAYE and IBR is less than the payment under the standard ten-year repayment plan.

Additional Notes & Details on PAYE

What if you no longer have a partial financial hardship?

For PAYE, you only need to show a PFH in the year you apply. Once you apply and are accepted, you will stay in PAYE whether or not you have a PFH in subsequent years.

Recertification

You must submit recertification every year to remain in PAYE or any income-driven repayment plan. This doesn't mean you need to have a PFH for recertification, just that you need to submit some paperwork to stay on the plan. If you forget to submit recertification for PAYE, your accrued interest will be capitalized, or added to the principal of your loan(s) (capped at 10 percent of the original loan amount), and you will be put on the standard ten-year repayment plan.

I will explain how to apply and submit recertification after we go through the details of the four income-driven repayment plans.

Accrued Interest

If you fail to recertify or no longer have a PFH,[23] any interest you accrued while on the PAYE repayment plan will be capitalized or added to the principal of your loan.

Regardless of how much interest has accrued, the maximum principal after capitalization is the original loan amount when you entered PAYE plus 10 percent.

If you're wondering what would cause you to have accrued interest, it's when your calculated monthly payment under PAYE is so low that it's not even enough to cover your monthly interest. Thankfully, most of the income-driven repayment plans have

---

23   You will not be moved off PAYE and onto a standard ten-year repayment plan simply because you no longer have a PFH, but your accrued interest will be added to the principal balance of your loan through capitalization. Whether you have a PFH or not, you still need to recertify every year to avoid being moved to the standard ten-year repayment plan.

an interest benefit that helps minimize the amount of interest that accrues.

Interest Benefit

Let's say you are in a scenario where your monthly payment under PAYE doesn't cover all the interest that is accruing on your loans. If this is the case, for the first three years of PAYE, the government covers any remaining interest on subsidized loans.

Payment Cap

Monthly payments under PAYE have a cap. They cannot exceed what your monthly payment would have been under the standard ten-year repayment plan for the amount of loans you had when you started PAYE. They will also never be more than 10 percent of your discretionary income, but they could be less due to the payment cap.

To refer back to our examples, Robert's monthly payment under PAYE will never be more than the $1,000 calculated payment under the standard ten-year repayment plan. In the same way, Charlie's monthly payment under PAYE will never be more than the $565 calculated payment under the standard ten-year repayment plan.

It makes sense to take a step back as we are talking about these income-driven repayment plans.

At the end of the day, it's important to know what your goal is. If your goal is to eventually pay back all your student loan debt, then a monthly payment that is lower than the standard ten-year payment is not ideal, because you will end up paying more in interest.

On the contrary, if your goal is to eventually have your loans forgiven, then a repayment plan like PAYE or REPAYE makes sense. It's also worth pointing out that you are allowed to make extra payments toward your student loans, regardless of what plan you are on.

Finally, it's worth pointing out that income-driven repayment may be the only way some people can afford to repay their student loans. For example, a single person who makes $38,000 a year but has $150,000 in student loans almost certainly needs to move onto an income-driven repayment plan simply to avoid defaulting on their loans. They may still have a desire to increase their income over time and pay off their loans entirely, but, in the short term, an income-driven plan is the right choice.

Revised Pay As You Earn (REPAYE)

The highlights of Revised Pay As You Earn (REPAYE):

- This is a newer plan that became available on December 16, 2015.

- Student loan payments are generally 10 percent of your discretionary income, though there is no cap on the required minimum payment (it can be more than what you would have paid on a standard ten-year repayment plan when you entered REPAYE).

- Partial loan forgiveness after 240 qualified payments, or twenty years, for undergraduate loans, and after 300 qualified payments, or twenty-five years, if repaying any graduate debt.

- No partial financial hardship (PFH) required.

- Loans from the Federal Direct Loan Program (FDLP) are the only loans that are eligible.

  Reminder: Parent PLUS loans and consolidation loans

that repaid Parent PLUS loans are *not eligible*. The only income-driven repayment plan these loans are eligible for is Income-Contingent Repayment (ICR).

- Your spouse's income affects the calculation, regardless of whether you file your taxes *jointly* or as *married filing separately*.

If you are not eligible for PAYE, REPAYE is a good option. There are some drawbacks compared to PAYE, the main one being that your spouse's income will be taken into consideration regardless of whether you file your taxes jointly or not. Nevertheless, REPAYE is still a good option.

As mentioned above, in REPAYE it doesn't matter whether you and your spouse file separate or joint tax returns; *all income is considered in the calculation*. This "marriage penalty" that comes with REPAYE can be viewed a couple of different ways. For borrowers, it's obviously not a positive thing because it penalizes them for getting married and rewards them for not getting married. From a taxpayer perspective, though, you could argue that the borrower has access to both incomes, not just their own, to repay student loans.

Recertification

Remember, you must submit recertification every year to remain in REPAYE or any income-driven repayment plan. If you forget to submit recertification, your accrued interest will be capitalized and you will be put on the standard ten-year repayment plan.

Accrued Interest

Like the PAYE repayment plan, if you fail to recertify, any interest you accrued while on the REPAYE repayment plan will be added to the principal of your loan through capitalization. The reason capitalization occurs when you do not recertify is that you will exit REPAYE and be put on the standard ten-year repayment plan. The only scenario wherein accrued interest is capitalized is when you leave the REPAYE plan for another plan, either voluntarily or by not submitting recertification.[24] If you stay in the plan (through annual recertification), your accrued interest will not be added to the principal balance of your loan(s).

If you forget to submit recertification and are moved off an income-driven repayment, you can always apply and get back on one. You will need a PFH to get back on PAYE and IBR, but a PFH is not required for REPAYE or ICR. This does not prevent your accrued interest from being added to the principal balance of your loan, though, as this happens whenever you move from an income-driven repayment plan to the standard ten-year repayment plan. You can see why there is a benefit to staying on an income-driven repayment plan by submitting your annual recertification each year.

Interest Benefit

REPAYE offers a solid interest benefit to borrowers. For the first three years of REPAYE, if your monthly payment under REPAYE doesn't cover all the interest that accrues for the month, the government covers any remaining interest on subsidized loans. This is a similar benefit to PAYE.

But there's more!

After three years, the government will pay half of any interest that your monthly payment doesn't cover on subsidized loans (the other half will accrue). The government will continue to cover that difference as long as your loans are in REPAYE.

And there's more!

---

24 More on accrued interest and other income-driven repayment plan topics here: https://studentaid.ed.gov/sa/repay-loans/understand/plans/income-driven

The government will pay half the difference of your unsubsidized loans during *all* periods of repayment under REPAYE. It's worth noting that REPAYE is the only income-driven repayment plan with an interest benefit for unsubsidized loans.

<u>Payment Cap</u>

Similar to PAYE, monthly payments under REPAYE are capped at 10 percent of discretionary income, though there is one distinct difference between PAYE and REPAYE. With PAYE, your monthly loan payment will never be higher than it would be under a standard ten-year repayment plan. As stated previously, this is not the case with REPAYE.

For example, let's say you and your partner's AGI was fifty thousand dollars for three years and then jumps to five hundred thousand dollars. Your new calculated monthly payment under REPAYE will be significantly higher than before.

Is this a bad thing? Not necessarily. Unless you are going to have your student loans forgiven through Public Service Loan Forgiveness or through the twenty or twenty-five years' worth of qualifying payments on REPAYE, you will save money by paying off your student loans faster.

If you find that your REPAYE payments have increased to more than they would be under the standard ten-year repayment plan, you could lower your monthly payment by exiting REPAYE and moving to the standard ten-year repayment plan. Any accrued interest will capitalize, though, if you exit REPAYE. My personal opinion is that you would be better off staying on REPAYE and making the higher payments.

The next two income-driven repayment plans we will cover are becoming less common, primarily because PAYE and REPAYE have more favorable terms. With that said, there are many borrowers already in these two plans, not to mention that one of the plans, ICR, is the only plan you can choose if you have a consolidation loan that includes a Parent PLUS loan.

Income-Based Repayment (IBR)

The highlights of IBR:

- You must have a partial financial hardship (PFH) in the year you apply.

- Partial loan forgiveness after 240 qualified payments, or twenty years, for new borrowers, and after 300 qualified payments, or twenty-five years, for those who are not new borrowers.

- Eligible "new" direct loan borrowers are eligible for a payment that is capped at 10 percent of discretionary income and for partial loan forgiveness after twenty years.

- To be an eligible "new" direct loan borrower for IBR, you must satisfy a couple of requirements: you have not taken out a federal direct loan prior to July 1, 2014 and have no outstanding balance on a FFEL program loan when you receive a direct loan on or after July 1, 2014.

- If you do not qualify as a "new" direct loan borrower, your payment is capped at 15 percent of discretionary income.

- Your monthly payment will never be more than what you would have paid under a standard ten-year repayment plan, based on what you owed when you entered IBR.

- Loans from the Federal Direct Loan Program (FDLP) and Federal Family Education Loan (FFEL) Program are eligible.

   Reminder: Parent PLUS loans and consolidation loans

that repaid Parent PLUS loans are *not eligible*. The only income-driven repayment plan these loans are eligible for are Income-Contingent Repayment (ICR).

- Your spouse's income affects the calculation, unless you file your taxes as *married filing separately*.

Recertification

Remember, you must submit recertification every year to remain in IBR or any income-driven repayment plan. If you forget to submit recertification, your accrued interest will be capitalized and you will be put on the standard ten-year repayment plan. Once you are on the standard ten-year repayment plan, you can apply to move back onto an income-driven repayment plan, but it won't "undo" any accrued interest that was already added to the principal of your loan.

Accrued Interest

If you fail to recertify or no longer have a PFH, any interest you accrued while on the IBR repayment plan will be added to the principal of your loan. Unlike PAYE, there is no cap to how much can be capitalized. And unlike REPAYE, capitalization isn't limited to scenarios where you exit the plan; it can be triggered simply by no longer having a PFH.

This is unforgiving compared to PAYE and REPAYE, and one reason why PAYE and REPAYE are becoming more popular than IBR.

Interest Benefit

For the first three years of IBR, if your monthly payment doesn't cover all the interest that accrues for the month, the government covers any remaining interest on subsidized loans. After three years, the interest benefit ends.

<u>Payment Cap</u>

Under IBR, payments are capped at either 10 percent or 15 percent of your discretionary income, depending on when you were a "new" borrower. If you were a new borrower on or after July 1, 2014, your payments are 10 percent of your discretionary income. Otherwise, your monthly payments will be 15 percent of your discretionary income.

Similar to PAYE, your monthly payment under IBR cannot exceed what your monthly payment would have been under the standard ten-year repayment plan for the amount of loans you had when you started IBR.

Income-Contingent Repayment (ICR)

The highlights of ICR:

- Loans from the Federal Direct Loan Program (FDLP), including Parent PLUS loans and consolidation loans that repaid Parent PLUS loans, are eligible.

- No partial financial hardship (PFH) required.

- Student loan payments are generally 20 percent of your discretionary income.

- When calculating discretionary income, ICR takes 100 percent of the federal poverty guideline into consideration, unlike the other income-driven repayment plans that take 150 percent into consideration.

- There is no cap on the required minimum payment (can be more than you would pay on a standard ten-year repayment plan).

- Partial loan forgiveness after 300 qualified payments, or twenty-five years.

- Your spouse's income affects the calculation, unless you file your taxes as *married filing separately*.

For various reasons, the ICR plan has become the least favorable income-driven repayment option. It does have one benefit over the other options, though: it's the only plan for which Parent PLUS loans and consolidation loans that repaid Parent PLUS loans are eligible.

Some of the negative aspects of ICR include the lack of an interest benefit and annual interest capitalization.

<u>Recertification</u>

Remember, you must submit recertification every year to remain in ICR or any income-driven repayment plan. If you forget to submit recertification, your accrued interest will be capitalized and you will be put on the standard ten-year repayment plan.

<u>Accrued Interest</u>

There is no interest benefit with ICR, which is unfortunate because any accrued interest is capitalized annually. There is a cap on accrued interest, though, as the annual capitalization will never be more than 10 percent of your original loan principal balance at the time you entered the ICR plan.

<u>Payment Cap</u>

As previously mentioned, under ICR, payments are generally 20 percent of your discretionary income. They can be less, though, if the amount that you would pay on a repayment plan with a fixed payment over the course of twelve years (adjusted according to your income) is less than the monthly payment calculated at 20 percent of your discretionary income. There is no cap on the required monthly payment; the payment can be more than you would pay on a standard ten-year repayment plan.

Income-Driven Repayment Application and Recertification

To apply for an income-driven repayment plan, you need to go to studentloans.gov and apply, or talk to your loan servicer(s). Studentloans.gov is also where you can change from one income-driven repayment plan to another and recertify each year.

Recertification is one of the most important aspects of income-driven repayment. Borrowers must resubmit the income-driven repayment application *each year* to recertify. Failing to do this prior to the deadline may cause your loans to shift to the standard ten-year repayment plan, which will also cause some or all of your accrued interest to be added to your loan balance through capitalization.

If you want to see a PDF of the income-driven repayment (IDR) plan request, you can view it here: https://static.studentloans. gov/images/idrPreview.pdf

Here is what part of the form looks like:

INCOME-DRIVEN REPAYMENT (IDR) PLAN REQUEST

For the Revised Pay As You Earn (REPAYE), Pay As You Earn (PAYE), Income-Based Repayment (IBR), and Income-Contingent Repayment (ICR) plans under the William D. Ford Federal Direct Loan (Direct Loan) Program and Federal Family Education Loan (FFEL) Programs

OMB No. 1845-0102
Form Approved
Exp. Date 10/31/2018

IDR

WARNING: Any person who knowingly makes a false statement or misrepresentation on this form or on any accompanying document is subject to penalties that may include fines, imprisonment, or both, under the U.S. Criminal Code and 20 U.S.C. 1097.

SECTION 1: BORROWER INFORMATION

Please enter or correct the following information.

☐ Check this box if any of your information has changed.

SSN	
Name	
Address	
City	State ____ Zip Code _____
Telephone - Primary	
Telephone - Alternate	
Email (Optional)	

SECTION 2: REPAYMENT PLAN OR RECERTIFICATION REQUEST

It's faster and easier to complete this form online at StudentLoans.gov. You can learn more at StudentAid.gov/IDR and by reading Sections 9 and 10. It's simple to get repayment estimates at StudentAid.gov/repayment-estimator. If you need help with this form, contact your loan holder or servicer for free assistance. You can find out who your loan holder or servicer is at StudentAid.gov/login. You may have to pay income tax on any loan amount forgiven under an income-driven plan.

1. **Select the reason you are submitting this form (Check only one):**
   ☐ I want to enter an income-driven plan - Continue to Item 2.
   ☐ I am submitting documentation for the annual

3. **Do you have multiple loan holders or servicers?**
   ☐ Yes - Submit a request to each holder or servicer. Continue to Item 4.
   ☐ No - Continue to item 4.

This form is used for a variety of purposes, including initially applying for an IDR plan as well as submitting an annual recertification of an IDR plan, as can be seen in question one:

1. Select the reason you are submitting this form (Check only one):

☐ I want to enter an income-driven plan - Continue to Item 2.

☐ I am submitting documentation for the annual recertification of my income-driven payment - Skip to Item 5.

☐ I am submitting documentation early to have my income-driven payment recalculated immediately - Skip to Item 5.

☐ I want to change to a different income-driven plan - Continue to Item 2.

Notice that option three is related to submitting documentation early to have your payment recalculated. Typically, if you are in a similar job and your income hasn't changed drastically, you would only submit this form once a year, for your annual recertification. But if you do find yourself in a new financial situation, such as staying home to raise children, making a career pivot into a lower-paying job, or any of a number of other changes, you can submit your recertification early and your required payment will be adjusted accordingly.

For example, let's say you submitted your annual recertification when your AGI was fifty thousand dollars. Soon after you submit that, you leave your job to stay home full-time. You can submit the annual recertification early and show that you have no income (assuming you have no side or part-time income). Unless you are on an IDR plan that requires your spouse's income to be factored in, if you file your tax returns separate from your spouse, your required monthly payment could be zero. Additionally, you will be on a path for loan forgiveness after twenty or twenty-five years, depending on your plan.[25]

Once you submit your application and move into an IDR plan, you will receive a disclosure and notice within a month. From there, it won't be until approximately the ninth month that you will receive a notice reminding you to recertify. The tenth month is a soft deadline to submit recertification, and the eleventh month is a hard deadline. By the end of the twelfth month, you must have submitted recertification, or you risk having your loans exit IDR.

---

25   It's important for me to say here that the fact that you are not required to make payments doesn't mean you should stop making voluntary payments. If you stop making payments, it's important you go "all in" on loan forgiveness and stick with the income-driven repayment plan for the long haul. Situations can change, and having student loan debt hanging over your head for twenty or twenty-five years is a tough pill to swallow. I would feel better if your partner was on board with making payments toward your student loans before you quit your job to stay home full-time.

What If I Don't Hear Back?

After submitting your application to move into an IDR plan, you should hear back within a couple of weeks. If you don't, here are a few things you can do:

Contact your Student Loan Servicer—Check with your loan servicer on the status of your application. If you receive no update, they seem unaware of your application, or in general you feel they are not being helpful in processing your application for IDR, move on to the next step.

Submit a Complaint to the Department of Education— You can submit complaints here: https://feedback. studentaid.ed.gov/

Submit a Complaint to the Consumer Financial Protection Bureau—You can submit complaints here: https://www. consumerfinance.gov/complaint/

Exiting your IDR plan has implications for loan forgiveness, especially if you are on a path to having your loans forgiven after twenty or twenty-five years.

Other Repayment Plans

The standard ten-year repayment plan and IDR plans are not the only options for federal student loan borrowers. There are also the Graduated Repayment Plan and the Extended Repayment Plan.

I left them to the end of the chapter, because these plans are becoming less popular. In fact, more likely than not, someone will move onto one of these plans by mistake, thinking the plan is eligible for loan forgiveness, which they are not...which is exactly why these plans are not popular and not recommended.

*The extended and graduated repayment plans
are not eligible for student loan forgiveness,
including Public Service Loan Forgiveness
and other forms of loan forgiveness.*

Nevertheless, I included the details of each. If you are on one of these plans, I would recommend moving to a standard ten-year repayment plan or an IDR plan.

To be eligible for the Extended Repayment Plan, you need at least thirty thousand dollars in direct loans or FFEL loans. The graduated repayment plan doesn't require you to have a certain amount of debt to qualify, so let's talk about that one first.

Graduated Repayment Plan

The logic behind the graduated repayment plan is that college grads will make more money over time. This is generally true, though the unfortunate impact of taking on the graduated repayment plan is that very little progress is made on your loans at the beginning, and each additional increase in your payment can be difficult to stomach.

Ten years is the repayment period under the graduated repayment plan for all loans other than consolidation loans. To have a repayment period for your consolidation loans that is greater than ten years, you must have a certain minimum balance to qualify. The below chart shows the minimum balance requirements (again, this is only for a Direct Consolidation Loan or FFEL Consolidation Loan):

Graduated Repayment Plans

Total Education Loan Indebtedness		Repayment period (years)
At Least	Less Than	
	$ 7,500	10
$ 7,500	$ 10,000	12
$ 10,000	$ 20,000	15
$ 20,000	$ 40,000	20
$ 40,000	$ 60,000	25
$ 60,000		30

Graduated repayment plans will vary by servicer, but typical characteristics include:

- Payments start out low and increase every two years.

- Payments are at least equal to the amount of interest that accrues on your loan each month (i.e. you may not make much or any progress on the principal of your loan in the first two years, but your payment will, at a minimum, cover the interest on your loan).

- Payments can't be more than three times greater than any other payment (meaning the final payment amount will not exceed the first payment amount by more than three times).

- The plan is structured to be paid off over the course of ten years, unless you have a Direct Consolidation Loan or FFEL Consolidation Loan, in which case you can potentially have a repayment period of up to thirty years.

Extended Repayment Plan

Extended repayment plans are similar to the standard ten-year repayment plan, as they have equal minimum payments throughout the life of the loan, just over a longer period of time. The actual extended schedules vary by loan servicer, but some of the common plans are twelve, fifteen, twenty, twenty-five, and thirty years.

There are a few requirements to qualify for an extended plan:

- For direct loans: You must have over $30,000 in outstanding direct loans and no outstanding balance on a direct Loan as of October 7, 1998.

- Likewise, for FFEL program loans: You must have over $30,000 in outstanding FFEL program loans and no outstanding balance on a FFEL program loan as of October 7, 1998.

- Example: If you have $50,000 in direct loans and $20,000 in FFEL program loans, your direct loans are eligible for Extended Repayment Plan, but the FFEL program loans are not.

Remember, extended and graduated repayment plans are not eligible for student loan forgiveness, including Public Service Loan Forgiveness. Weigh your options carefully before you go this route.

Estimate your monthly payment under various repayment plans using the studentloans.gov tool.[26]

If you log in using your FSA ID, your loan information can be automatically loaded in, or you can enter it manually (use the data from the spreadsheet you created in step one).

Let's walk through an example using the following assumptions:

$40,000 direct subsidized loans

$60,000 direct unsubsidized loans

6.5 percent interest rate on all loans

Single with no dependents, residing in the state of Minnesota

$35,000 AGI

Here are the results we get:

----

26   The full URL: https://studentloans.gov/myDirectLoan/repaymentEstimator.action

Standard You will pay a total of **$136,258** over **120 months**	$1,135 - $1,135/month	⊕
Graduated You will pay a total of **$146,145** over **120 months**	$653 - $1,958/month	⊕
Extended Fixed You will pay a total of **$202,562** over **300 months**	$675 - $675/month	⊕
Extended Graduated You will pay a total of **$219,792** over **300 months**	$542 - $983/month	⊕
Revised Pay As You Earn (REPAYE) You will pay a total of **$105,754** over **300 months**	$140 - $673/month	⊕
Pay As You Earn (PAYE) You will pay a total of **$69,760** over **240 months**	$140 - $499/month	⊕
Income-Based Repayment (IBR) You will pay a total of **$158,631** over **300 months**	$210 - $1,010/month	⊕
IBR for New Borrowers You will pay a total of **$69,760** over **240 months**	$140 - $499/month	⊕
Income-Contingent Repayment (ICR) You will pay a total of **$234,624** over **300 months**	$381 - $1,092/month	⊕

When using this tool, don't let the wide range distract you. Instead, **focus on the lower amount in the range**. That amount is what you are estimated to pay today.

The reason there is a range of payments is that the tool assumes 3 percent growth in AGI each year. The calculations are relatively complicated, so I can't fault the Department of Education for simplifying the tool using this variable. The range they are providing, in some cases, is over the course of twenty or twenty-five years. Your income likely isn't going to increase by 3 percent every year, consistently.

This tool also allows you to see projected payments and forgiveness under Public Service Loan Forgiveness (PSLF) which, under certain conditions, allows you to have eligible student loans forgiven after 120 qualifying payments. All you have to do is toggle the option that enables this.

Show payment estimated under Public Service Loan Forgiveness (PSLF) ❓

Here's our new breakout of the various repayment plans when PSLF is considered.

Standard You will pay a total of **$136,258** over **120 months**	$1,135 - $1,135/month	➕
Graduated You will pay a total of **$146,145** over **120 months**	$653 - $1,958/month	➕
Extended Fixed You will pay a total of **$202,562** over **300 months**	$675 - $675/month	➕
Extended Graduated You will pay a total of **$219,792** over **300 months**	$542 - $983/month	➕
Revised Pay As You Earn (REPAYE) You will pay a total of **$23,745** over **120 months**	$140 - $265/month	➕
Pay As You Earn (PAYE) You will pay a total of **$23,745** over **120 months**	$140 - $265/month	➕
Income-Based Repayment (IBR) You will pay a total of **$35,618** over **120 months**	$210 - $397/month	➕
IBR for New Borrowers You will pay a total of **$23,745** over **120 months**	$140 - $265/month	➕
Income-Contingent Repayment (ICR) You will pay a total of **$61,009** over **120 months**	$381 - $655/month	➕

As you can see, for those with a high level of loans and relatively lower income, PSLF can potentially save tens of thousands—or, in some cases, hundreds of thousands—of dollars.

Let's dive into loan forgiveness now.

Everything You Need to Know about Loan Forgiveness

Perhaps you pay two hundred dollars a month in student loans. Or five hundred dollars. Or more.

Now imagine not having to pay *anything* toward student loans. Imagine they are completely gone.

What would you do without student loans hanging over you? How would you use that extra money? Would you save for a house? A car? A trip?

How would you feel?

Student loans weigh on millions of Americans. Many are desperate for a path to have them eliminated and feel they will be paying student loans forever.

I'm happy to say that, in the midst of all the negativity that surrounds student loans, there is one silver lining: Most federal student loans have a path to forgiveness. It will take anywhere from ten to twenty-five years, but the opportunity is there.

No more student loans? Tell me how!

Before we get too excited, there are a few things to keep in mind:

- Student loan forgiveness requires diligent, on-time monthly payments and annual recertification for the opportunity to have loans forgiven after ten, twenty, or twenty-five years.

- Mistakes like being in the wrong repayment plan, missing an annual recertification, or missing a required minimum monthly payment can be detrimental or, in some cases, catastrophic. When this happens, your twenty or twenty-five-year timeline to forgiveness can be reset, accrued interest added to the balance of your loan, and your loans put back on the standard ten-year repayment plan.

- The government can technically change the rules at any time. Thankfully, there are now advocacy groups specifically focused on student loan debt who push back whenever forgiveness programs are threatened.

- Other than Public Service Loan Forgiveness (PSLF), you most likely will pay taxes on the amount forgiven. It takes preparation to be ready for this tax bill.

- To be blunt, twenty to twenty-five years, which is the timeline for loan forgiveness if you aren't pursuing PSLF, is a really long time.

On a more positive note, if you read older books or articles on student loan forgiveness, many point out the fact that no one has actually had their loans forgiven through these programs. This is no longer the case.

There are now documented cases of individuals who have had their loans discharged through Public Service Loan Forgiveness. Michael Mitchell was one of the first when he had $170,000 of student loans wiped clean by the federal government, tax-free.[27]

---

27   You can read about it in this *New York Times* article: "Public Servants Do Get Student Loan Forgiveness. Meet One of the First." https://www.nytimes.com/2018/05/04/your-money/student-loan-forgiveness.html. May 2018.

Why Can't I Just Declare Bankruptcy?

The first thing most people think of when it comes to getting rid of debt is bankruptcy. Unfortunately, student loans are incredibly difficult to discharge in bankruptcy. If bankruptcy were an option, I imagine many would jump at the opportunity. After all, if you graduate with seventy-five thousand dollars of debt with little savings or assets, why not declare bankruptcy and get yourself out of a seventy-five-thousand-dollar hole?

To play devil's advocate, you can see how this would be troublesome. After all, a college degree is an investment in your future. On average, someone with a college degree makes significantly more over the course of their working life than someone who doesn't. By allowing borrowers to discharge their student loans in bankruptcy court, the lender (in most cases, the federal government) would be left holding the bag, even if the borrower goes on to make a reasonable income that could have, in theory, helped them pay off their student loans.

But these arguments don't help your specific situation, and it's not normal for debt to have little to no recourse in bankruptcy. If you declare bankruptcy, other debt such as credit card debt or personal loans can be discharged, but this is not the case with student loans.

Needless to say, this inability to get rid of student loan debt weighs on borrowers. You may have student loans from a degree you never finished. Or you may be working in a field that is totally unrelated to what you went to college for. You may even regret going to college and taking out loans in the first place.

Thankfully, the federal government has set up avenues for student loan forgiveness. If you read the previous section on repayment options, this won't be a surprise to you, because I highlighted the timeline for student loan forgiveness for each of the IDR plans.

The major opportunities for student loan forgiveness include:

- Public Service Loan Forgiveness (PSLF)
- Loan Forgiveness through IDR Plans
- Teacher Loan Forgiveness
- Other Types of Loan Forgiveness

Not surprisingly, these opportunities differ significantly in terms of requirements and timeline. They even differ in terms of how they are treated from a tax perspective.

Let's start by taking a look at Public Service Loan Forgiveness, which I anticipate will become very popular over the next decade if the cost of college continues to rise as it has been.

Have private student loans?

Unfortunately, private student loans are not eligible for loan forgiveness programs. There are a ton of tips and hacks in this book that will help you optimize your finances and eliminate your debt. If your only loans are private loans, skip ahead to Step Three: *Your Money–Understand Your Financial Situation.*

If your payments are so high that you are struggling to repay your loans, consider refinancing for a longer term or renegotiating your payment plan with your current lender.

Public Service Loan Forgiveness (PSLF)

Public Service Loan Forgiveness, or PSLF, is the most popular and financially advantageous way to have your student loans forgiven. For some, PSLF alone could potentially justify working at a qualified nonprofit organization over a private company.

Here are the high-level details of PSLF:

- You must be on a qualified repayment plan:
  - Ten-year Standard Plan
  - REPAYE
  - PAYE
  - IBR
  - ICR

- The only qualifying loans are:
  - Direct Subsidized
  - Direct Unsubsidized
  - Direct Graduate PLUS
  - Direct Parent PLUS (only if consolidated through a Direct Consolidation Loan)
  - Direct Consolidation

- The only qualifying employers are:
  - Government organizations at all levels (state, federal, etc.)
  - Not-for-profit organizations that are tax-exempt under section 501(c)(3) of the Internal Revenue Code
  - Other types of not-for-profit organizations that are not tax-exempt under section 501(c)(3) of the Internal Revenue Code, if their primary purpose is to provide certain types of qualifying public services

- You must make 120 qualifying payments while on a qualified repayment plan and working for a qualifying employer.

- You can stop and start PSLF; it does *not* have to be 120 consecutive payments.

- You must submit the appropriate paperwork—the burden of proof will always fall on the borrower. Keep all your documentation.

- You must still work in public service when you apply for and receive forgiveness.

- Any loans forgiven through PSLF are tax-free.

- FFEL, Perkins, loans in default, and private student loans are not eligible for PSLF.

Eligible Repayment Plans

The first thing that may stand out is the fact that a standard ten-year repayment plan is an eligible plan for PSLF. After ten years on this plan, though, and 120 qualifying payments, your loans would be paid off. What's the deal?

One scenario where this would matter is for someone who worked for an eligible employer for a few years and did not know about IDR plans or PSLF. If they worked for an eligible employer, there is potential that the payments made on the standard ten-year repayment plan while working for that employer would count toward their 120. They could then switch to an IDR plan, lower their payment, and, after they hit the 120 qualifying payments, have their remaining eligible student loans forgiven.

Keep in mind that there are repayment plans that are *ineligible* for PSLF, or any type of loan forgiveness for that matter. They include any graduated repayment or extended-term repayment plans. A good rule of thumb is that you will want to be in an IDR plan if you are pursuing PSLF.

Qualifying Payments

There are five conditions for a payment to be qualified for PSLF.[28] The payment must have been made...

- after October 1, 2007
- under a qualifying repayment plan
- for the full amount due, as shown on your bill
- no later than fifteen days after your due date
- while you were employed full-time by a qualifying employer[29]

You can always pay extra toward your student loans, but it doesn't "speed up" PSLF. For example, if your required monthly payment under your IDR plan was $150 but, in a given month, you paid an extra $150 for a total of $300, this does not count for more than one eligible payment. Only one eligible payment can be made per month.

Additionally, if the extra $150 was marked as early payment for next month's required payment, you just missed out on an eligible payment. Is your head spinning yet?

The reason why you miss out on an eligible payment by paying next month's required payment early is that you can't receive

---

28   As explained here: https://studentaid.ed.gov/sa/repay-loans/forgiveness-cancellation/public-service#qualifying-employment

29   Technically this can be two (or more) part-time jobs, as long as the hours end up being equivalent to "full time" (forty hours). Employers would all need to be qualifying employers and employer certification would need to be submitted for each.

credit for making an eligible payment if there is no required payment in a given month. By paying next month's required payment early, you no longer have a required payment next month. You can't receive credit for making a qualified payment in a month where there was no required payment due.

You can only make qualified payments in months in which you are required to make a payment. For example, if you are in deferment, forbearance, or a grace period or have in-school status, you cannot make qualifying payments.

This comes into play for many graduate students who have a required six-month grace period. You may be employed at an eligible employer right out of school, but your first six months do not count toward PSLF because you are not yet required to make payments and therefore cannot make qualified payments, even if you voluntarily make payments toward your student loans right out of school.[30]

Bottom line: You can only be given credit for one qualifying payment per month. You can pay extra, but you will need to make sure your loan servicer does not apply it to future months' required payments.

A better solution: put whatever extra money you have toward a savings or investment account instead of toward your loans. After all, you are working toward PSLF, so paying off your loans faster typically is not beneficial.

Qualifying Employment

The employment requirement for PSLF is important. Qualifying employers must fit within one of these three categories:

---

30   One way around this is by consolidating your loans while in the grace period.

1) Government organizations at any level (federal, state, local, or tribal)

If you work for a government organization, you are eligible for PSLF.

An important caveat to this is that government contractors may not qualify. For example, let's say your for-profit employer provides services for a contract they have with the federal government. You are not directly employed by the government and, even if you are referred to as a "government contractor," your employment is with a for-profit employer. In this case, you are not eligible for PSLF.

One group of government employees who can benefit from PSLF is teachers. It's a widely held opinion that teachers, counselors, and other public servants employed by the government are underpaid. There are many public-school teachers who piled on student loans and find themselves in a difficult financial situation because of it. By switching to an IDR plan, keeping the appropriate records and documentation for PSLF, and making smart money moves, teachers can put themselves in a good financial position and have their student loan debt discharged tax-free after ten years.

2) Not-for-profit organizations that are tax-exempt under Section 501(c)(3) of the Internal Revenue Code

If you work for a nonprofit and have no idea how you are going to get rid of your student loans on your current salary, don't despair—there's a good chance you are eligible for PSLF.

There are exceptions to this. Employment with a labor union or partisan political organization is *not* eligible employment for PSLF. PSLF eligibility may also be in jeopardy if you work for a religious organization, depending on the nature of your job. Any time spent on religious instruction, worship services, or proselytizing does not count as eligible hours toward PSLF. Because you need to work the equivalent of what your employer would define as full-time hours (typically forty hours a week), or thirty or more hours, whichever is greater, the government could have grounds for denying PSLF even if only a small portion of your weekly work is spent on religious instruction, worship services, or proselytizing.

3) Other types of not-for-profit organizations that are not tax-exempt under Section 501(c)(3) of the Internal Revenue Code, if their primary purpose is to provide certain types of qualifying public services

Applying for PSLF is easier if your employer is a not-for-profit that is tax-exempt under section 501(c)(3) of the Internal Revenue Code but, even if your employer isn't tax-exempt, this doesn't necessarily mean you do not qualify. If the primary function of the not-for-profit is one of the following services, you may still work for an eligible employer:

- Emergency management
- Military service
- Public safety
- Law enforcement
- Public interest legal services
- Early childhood education
- Public service for individuals with disabilities
- Public service for the elderly
- Public health
- Public education
- Public library services

- School library services
- Other school-based services

The PSLF Employment Certification Form[31] provides additional clarifying details for some of these categories.

The Application Process for PSLF

If you think that you qualify for PSLF, here are the steps to take:

1. Apply for an IDR plan.

2. Submit the PSLF Employment Certification Form.

3. Submit the Employee Certification Form annually (a good habit to get into is submitting this at the same time you submit your annual IDR plan certification).

4. After you make 120 qualifying payments, submit the PSLF Application for Forgiveness.[32]

I may sound like a broken record, but you need to recertify annually to stay in an IDR plan.

You should also resubmit the Employment Certification Form annually or whenever you change employers. While not required, it's best to send this document in annually and keep it for your records. Another reason it's a good idea to resubmit this annually is that it needs to be signed by an official within your organization. Nonprofits do shut down—my wife worked for a nonprofit that no longer exists—and it may become difficult to track down an official to sign the form. Note that if you are unable to obtain certification from your employer, it does not mean your PSLF payments will not count. The Department of

---

31   The Employment Certification Form can be found here: https://studentaid.ed.gov/sa/
      sites/default/files/public-service-employment-certification-form.pdf

32   The PSLF Application for Forgiveness form can be found here: https://studentaid.
      ed.gov/sa/sites/default/files/public-service-application-for-forgiveness.pdf

Education will help in these situations but, obviously, it's ideal if they can simply be avoided.

Below is what the first page of the Employment Certification Form looks like:

PUBLIC SERVICE LOAN FORGIVENESS (PSLF):
EMPLOYMENT CERTIFICATION FORM
William D. Ford Federal Direct Loan (Direct Loan) Program

OMB No. 1845-0110
Form Approved
Exp. Date 5/31/2020
PSECF - XBCR

WARNING: Any person who knowingly makes a false statement or misrepresentation on this form or on any accompanying document is subject to penalties that may include fines, imprisonment, or both, under the U.S. Criminal Code and 20 U.S.C. 1097.

PSLF ECF

SECTION 1: BORROWER INFORMATION

Please enter or correct the following information.
☐ **Check this box if any of your information has changed.**

SSN	
Date of Birth	
Name	
Address	
City	State Zip Code
Telephone - Primary	
Telephone - Alternate	
Email (Optional)	

SECTION 2: BORROWER AUTHORIZATIONS, UNDERSTANDINGS, AND CERTIFICATION

Before signing, carefully read the entire form. For more information on PSLF, visit StudentAid.gov/publicservice.
I authorize:

1. My employer or other entity having records about the employment that is the basis of my request to make information from those records available to the U. S. Department of Education (the Department) or its agents or contractors.

2. The entity to which I submit this request and its agents to contact me regarding my request or my loans at any cellular telephone number that I provide now or in the future using automated telephone dialing equipment or artificial or prerecorded voice or text messages.

When you submit your Employment Certification Form, the Department of Education will verify that your employer is qualified. At that point, all your loans with the Department of Education will transfer to FedLoan Servicing, which has the exclusive right to manage PSLF borrowers' accounts. FedLoan Servicing determines how many qualified payments were made during the time frame you submitted on your application.

Submitting Your Application for Forgiveness

Once you have submitted 120 qualifying payments for PSLF, it's time to submit your Application for Forgiveness.

The Application for Forgiveness looks fairly similar to the Application for Employment Certification. You can view it at studentaid.gov.[33]

PSLF APP

PUBLIC SERVICE LOAN FORGIVENESS (PSLF):
APPLICATION FOR FORGIVENESS
William D. Ford Federal Direct Loan (Direct Loan) Program

OMB No. 1845-0110
Form Approved
Exp. Date 5/31/2020
PSFAP - XBCR

WARNING: Any person who knowingly makes a false statement or misrepresentation on this form or on any accompanying document is subject to penalties that may include fines, imprisonment, or both, under the U.S. Criminal Code and 20 U.S.C. 1097.

SECTION 1: BORROWER INFORMATION

Please enter or correct the following information.
☐ **Check this box if any of your information has changed.**

SSN
Date of Birth
Name
Address
City _____ State _____ Zip Code
Telephone - Primary
Telephone - Alternate
Email (Optional)

For more information on PSLF, visit StudentAid.gov/publicservice. Use this form only if you **(1)** have Direct Loans, **(2)** made 120 qualifying payments on the Direct Loans for which you are seeking forgiveness, and **(3)** worked, and continue to work, full-time at a qualifying employer when you made the qualifying payments. If the employment certified in this application and/or prior approved Employment Certification Forms does not cover all 120 qualifying payments, you must submit an employment certification for each qualifying employer that covers the rest of your qualifying payments.

SECTION 2: BORROWER REQUEST, UNDERSTANDINGS, CERTIFICATION, AND AUTHORIZATION

I request (1) that the U.S. Department of Education (the Department) forgive the remaining balance of my Direct Loans and **(2)** if I submit employment certification covering 10 years of qualifying employment after October 1, 2007, a forbearance on my Direct Loans while the Department determines my eligibility for forgiveness, unless I indicate otherwise below.
☐ By checking this box, I am indicating that I **do not want a forbearance** while my application is being processed.

Remember, *you must work for an eligible employer when submitting your Application for Forgiveness.* If you plan on changing employers, try to avoid doing so while your application is being processed. Wait until after your balance has been wiped clean.

When you apply, your loans will be put in forbearance unless you check the box that indicates you do not want this done while your application is being processed. Continue to make payments during this time.

---

33 You can see the form here: https://studentaid.ed.gov/sa/sites/default/files/public-service-application-for-forgiveness.pdf

If your application is accepted, you will receive notification and your loan balances on FedLoan will be zero.

If your application is rejected, you will be notified of the reasons why. If additional documentation is requested, provide it. If you think a mistake has been made and your application has been rejected in error, don't let up—be persistent. Don't hesitate to reach out to a lawyer or other professional if needed.

With the combination of wage stagnation and ever-higher student loan balances, PSLF will become more common.

Here are a few strategies I recommend implementing if you are working toward PSLF:

- **Keep all documentation**—It's important to keep all documentation of where you worked, when you worked, and annual IDR recertification submissions and employer certification submissions.

  Print out and keep paper copies. Keep backup electronic copies on the cloud and on a hard drive. Yes, this may be overdoing it but, with so much money on the line, you should cover your bases.

- **Adjusted Gross Income**—Under IDR, adjusted gross income is what matters. It determines how much you will pay each month (along with family size). Keeping your AGI low by investing in tax-advantaged retirement accounts is generally a good move. We'll talk more about this later in the book.

- **Spouse's Income**—If you are on REPAYE, focusing on your finances alone won't cut it; you need to think about what your spouse's income is and where it's going. If you and your partner's combined AGI is too high for IDR, PSLF may not make sense and you should instead focus on paying off your student loans as quickly as possible.[34]

Loan Forgiveness through IDR Plans

If you aren't eligible for PSLF, you can still have your student loans forgiven; the timeline is just significantly longer, either twenty or twenty-five years, depending on several factors.

The first step is the same as if you were pursuing PSLF: get into an IDR plan.

> **PAYE**—Partial loan forgiveness after 240 qualified payments, or twenty years.

> **REPAYE**—Partial loan forgiveness after 240 qualified payments, or twenty years, for undergraduate loans, and after 300 qualified payments, or twenty-five years, if repaying any graduate debt (including a consolidation loan that repaid a graduate student loan).

> **IBR**—Partial loan forgiveness after 240 qualified payments, or twenty years, for new direct loan borrowers, and after 300 qualified payments, or twenty-five years, for those who are not new direct loan borrowers.

> What's a "new" borrower? A new direct loan borrower as of July 1, 2014 (with no outstanding balance on a FFEL Program loan when you receive a direct loan on or after July 1, 2014).

---

34 When I say pay off your student loans as quickly as possible, I do not mean that other financial goals should take a back seat. For example, if you do not have an emergency fund, or if you have high-interest credit card debt, these should take priority. Read more about this in step three.

ICR—Partial loan forgiveness after 300 qualified payments, or twenty-five years.

A couple of important notes:

- Always validate that your payment went through on time each month. Failure to pay on time could cause your loan to be moved out of IDR and back to the standard ten-year repayment plan, which resets your twenty- or twenty-five-year loan forgiveness clock. Brutal![35]

- Student loans that are forgiven this way are not tax-free. For example, if you get one hundred thousand dollars of your student loans forgiven by the government, you will have to report that one hundred thousand dollars as taxable income. You need to prepare financially for the potentially large tax bill heading your way. Leverage your lower student loan payments to build up savings and investments that can eventually help cover the expected tax bill.

Teacher Loan Forgiveness

If you're a teacher, you are in luck—there is a whole additional set of forgiveness programs that you are eligible for in addition to PSLF. Teacher Loan Forgiveness, or TLF, offers either $5,000 or $17,500 of loan forgiveness, depending on your qualifications.

$5,000 teacher forgiveness

---

35 Unlike Public Service Loan Forgiveness, you cannot start and stop the process for twenty- or twenty-five-year forgiveness. You need to stay in an income-driven repayment plan for twenty or twenty-five years straight to receive forgiveness on eligible loans. **If you miss a payment or forget to recertify each year, you risk your forgiveness clock starting over completely**. You will be put back on the standard ten-year repayment plan, and, at that time, you can move back onto an income-driven repayment plan, but your loan forgiveness clock starts over completely.

- Full-time, highly-qualified teacher for five consecutive years after October 1, 1998

- Low-income school or education service agency

- Elementary/secondary school

$17,500 teacher forgiveness

- Full-time, highly-qualified teacher for five consecutive years after October 1, 1998

- Low-income school or education service agency

- Secondary school

- Math, science, and special education teachers only

TLF has one big drawback: you can't double-dip with PSLF. Based on the requirements of TLF and the fact that many have more than $5,000 or $17,500 in student loans, working toward PSLF usually makes more sense. Plus, with TLF, you have to meet strict requirements year after year, such as working in a low-income school.

Another benefit of PSLF over TLF is that TLF requires you to be a full-time teacher for five consecutive years at an eligible school or education service agency. There's always a risk that budget cuts will ruin a teacher's ability to be eligible for TLF by forcing them to consider employment at a non-eligible school or a move down to part-time work. You can leverage two or more part-time jobs to fulfill the full-time equivalent requirement of PSLF. You also do not have to make consecutive eligible payments, making disruptions caused by budget cuts less important.

Other Types of Loan Forgiveness

Public Service Loan Forgiveness, Teacher Loan Forgiveness, and the PSLF alternative of twenty or twenty-five years of repayment on an IDR plan are the most popular loan forgiveness options, but they are not the only ones. Here are a few additional opportunities for discharging student loan debt, which is the more popular terminology for these specific opportunities.

- **Total and Permanent Disability (TPD) Discharge—** TPD Discharge is a student loan forgiveness program through the federal government that discharges federal student loans for those deemed totally and permanently disabled. This process can be kicked off in a few ways, including submitting a certification from a doctor of medicine (MD) or osteopath (DO) that you are totally and permanently disabled. There is much more that can be said about this program, but, in reality, only a small percentage of student loan borrowers will be eligible.[36]

- **Closed School Discharge—**One day you are going to classes, and the next day your school is closed. This is a scenario no one wants to find themselves in, and it creates all kinds of issues. If you were enrolled in a school when it closed, were on an approved leave of absence when it closed, or withdrew within 120 days of a school closing, you may be eligible for 100 percent discharge of your federal student loans.[37]

- **Borrower Defense to Repayment Loan Forgiveness—**If you took out federal student loans to attend a school that misled you or engaged in other misconduct in violation of certain state laws, you may

---

36 More about TPD Discharge: https://www.disabilitydischarge.com/
37 More about closed school discharge: https://studentaid.ed.gov/sa/repay-loans/forgiveness-cancellation/closed-school

be eligible for student loan forgiveness under borrower defense. To put it plainly, if a school made fraudulent and/or misleading claims about something like future employment opportunities, you may have support for borrower defense.[38]

There are other opportunities for loan forgiveness along these lines, but these are a few of the major ones. A hot topic at the time of this writing was fraud surrounding for-profit colleges. If you feel you were a victim of fraudulent claims made by a school, by all means look into your options for loan forgiveness.

There are also one-off programs for partial student loan forgiveness. For example, the National Health Service Corps Loan Repayment Program offers primary care medical, dental, and mental and behavioral health care providers the opportunity to have their student loans repaid, in exchange for providing health care in communities with limited access to care.[39] Two years of full-time work qualify you for either fifty or twenty-five thousand dollars of loan forgiveness, based on the need of the community served. They have a part-time option as well. Another perk of this forgiveness program is that you can use it more than once, potentially allowing you to repay all your loans if you continue to serve in an eligible community.

Key Takeaways

- Private student loans have fewer repayment options than federal student loans and are not eligible for IDR or student loan forgiveness. Prioritize paying off your private student loans over your federal student loans.

---

38   More about borrower defense: https://studentaid.ed.gov/sa/repay-loans/forgiveness-cancellation/borrower-defense

39   More information here: https://nhsc.hrsa.gov/

- Proceed with caution if you are considering refinancing your federal student loans. It could save you thousands of dollars in interest, but it also results in the loss of the ability to enroll in IDR plans and loan forgiveness.

- Always make the minimum required monthly payment on your loans.

- IDR plans can make your monthly payments more affordable, capping payment at 10–20 percent of your discretionary income.

- Forbearance and deferment can result in accrued interest being added to the principal through the process of capitalization. Make sure you understand the implications of forbearance and deferment on your loans before taking advantage of either.

- When you are behind on student loan payments but haven't defaulted, you can use deferment or forbearance to make your loans current.

- You can exit default through loan rehabilitation or loan consolidation.

- Public Service Loan Forgiveness (PSLF) can be a big financial win for those who are eligible, providing tax-free loan forgiveness after 120 qualifying payments.

- Use the studentaid.gov repayment tool to analyze what you would pay under different repayment plans, as well as to estimate how much you may have forgiven under PSLF.

Step 3:

Your Money–Understand Your Financial Situation

You made it.

It's not easy to understand student loans. Yes, at the core, they are simple: it's debt—and you need to repay it.

But it's not that simple, especially if you have federal student loans.

Step three is not about the ins and outs of student loans. It's about you. Your financial life. How much money you make. How much money you spend, and on what.

Do you have an emergency fund? Do you need one? We'll discuss.

Should you be investing or prioritizing paying off debt? We'll discuss.

And what if you have other debt, like credit cards or a car loan? Which do you pay off first? How do you avoid drowning in debt? You guessed it: We'll discuss.

In this step, you will gain an understanding of where you are right now. The good, the bad, and the ugly. Remember, we are pursuing *control over your financial life*. Understanding your loans and repayment options were the first steps, but we need to couple that with your *specific situation*.

This is why we will wait until step four to actually pick a strategy and plan for your student loans. We can't pick the best plan without first knowing where you are. Then, in step five, we will talk about how to optimize your finances, which is truly a never-ending process that you can work at over time.

Track Your Money—Income, Expenses, and Cash Flow

Anyone who wants control over their money needs to understand how much they are making, spending, and saving. But this is even more important if you have student loans. Having one hundred dollars, five hundred dollars, or even more going toward student loans every month means you need to make sure you are making the best use of whatever money you have left over.

If you don't know what you're spending your money on, you will never be in control of your money. It's that simple.

You've probably heard that budgeting is key to managing your money. You may even budget already. While budgeting is essential, there is an important first step to take *before* budgeting: tracking your income and expenses.

I'm going to assume you don't already track your spending each month. If that's the case, you could start today and, in a few months, you would have a good idea of how much, on average, you spend each month. But we don't have time to pause everything and wait three months. After all, we're trying to create a student loan strategy *now*.

Instead, we are going to take advantage of the fact that most transactions today are digital. This makes it easier to look up your spending from the past three months and use that as a gauge of how much you spend.

- -

Gather the past three months of income and spending data from your credit card and bank statements.

You can use the budget spreadsheet found here: StudentLoanSolutionBook.com. There are two budget spreadsheets available, one that is simple and one that is a bit more advanced that uses an automation tool to pull in your transactions in a uniform format. Each spreadsheet has directions on how to add your data from the last few months.

If you dislike or struggle with spreadsheets, you can do all of this with pen and paper. In fact, I even created some printables that will make this a little easier.[40]

For each of the past three months, assign all your spending to specific categories. This *will* take some time, but it's important information to have. And you'll just have to trust me that digging into your finances at this level can be rewarding.

Add up all your income and expenses each month and see how much money is left over, or how much more you spent than you brought in.

Some common categories to group your expenses are:

- Auto
- Insurance (Auto, Health, Life)
- Cable and Internet
- Car Loan
- Cell Phone
- Clothes
- Donations/Charity
- Entertainment
- Transportation

---

40   You guessed it, you can find the printables here: StudentLoanSolutionBook.com

- Gifts

- Groceries

- Gym

- Haircuts

- Health Care (Doctor Visits, Prescriptions, etc.)

- Household Goods, Furniture, etc.

- Rent/Mortgage

- Pets

- Restaurants/Drinks

- School (Tuition, Books, Supplies)

- Student Loans

- Toiletries

- Travel

- Utilities

In this initial look back at the past three months, you may miss some cash transactions, but they are likely minimal. Going forward, you should record these transactions in your phone and transfer them to your budget spreadsheet, app, or printed-out budget templates later.

Once you have gathered your spending data from the past three months, it's time to analyze it. Below are a few questions to ask yourself and work through. Try not to overthink or overanalyze. Just get your initial thoughts down.

Are you spending more than you make? If so, are there certain categories that are driving you to spend too much? Or is your take-home income too low?

_____

_____

_____

_____

_____

Were there any spending categories that surprised you? For example, are you spending five hundred dollars a month on groceries when you thought you were only spending three hundred?

_____

_____

_____

_____

_____

How much of your income (both amount and percent) is going toward student loans? How much would this decrease, if any, under an IDR plan (this was estimated at the end of step two for your federal loans)?

_____

_____

_____

_____

_____

If you are spending more than you make, it could be an income problem, a spending problem, or both. After all, there are athletes who made millions who went bankrupt. In their case, it's pretty obvious that they had a spending problem.

Nearly everyone has opportunities to cut spending and increase their income. My entire book *Hustle Away Debt* focuses on how to make money above and beyond your nine-to-five job. While I'm all about increasing income and putting that extra money to work, cutting spending may be easier.

Making an extra three hundred dollars a month through a side hustle can be much more difficult than making an extra three hundred dollars by cutting costs. For example, purchasing an eight-thousand-dollar car instead of a twenty-thousand-dollar car would result in a lower monthly payment. Making a decision like this can be easier than finding a way to increase your income to justify the twenty-thousand-dollar car.

In step five, we'll go through the process of creating a monthly budget and discuss ways to limit your spending and increase your income.

For now, though, the key piece of information is how much extra money—or lack thereof—you have at the end of the month, on average. We'll use this information when picking your repayment strategy in step four.

Now, let's talk about what I think is one of the most important topics in personal finance: the emergency fund.

Ready for an Emergency?

For the first couple of years my wife and I were out of college, money was the cause of a lot of stress. We had "okay" income for being fresh out of college, but we also had a huge student loan bill due each month (I was clueless at the time that there were income-driven repayment plans). We both had plans to get master's degrees, and the thought of taking on additional debt stressed us out. Every unexpected bill felt more devastating than it should have. Conversations around money were not always healthy or rational.

When I'm faced with a problem, I like to take action. When I look back at everything I have done to improve my finances since that low point, there is one thing that had a huge positive impact: **establishing an emergency fund**.

For most people, building an emergency fund is difficult. There is a list of things that constantly demand your money. Whether it's your student loan debt or other debt, bills, groceries, Christmas presents, or any other number of things, there will always be something you could use money for.

With all these demands on your money, how could you possibly build an emergency fund, especially three to six months' worth of expenses?

I've been there. Establishing and growing an emergency fund can be daunting. The key is to start *somewhere*.

First of all, you need positive cash flow. This may require moving your student loans into a different repayment plan to lower your monthly payment, refinancing your credit card debt into a personal loan, or taking drastic measures like moving into more affordable housing. Or it could be smaller moves, like being more conscientious of what you spend your money on.

My wife and I took a variety of actions to build an emergency fund. Among other things, we increased our income through side hustles[41] and started couponing. We were more thoughtful about the money we spent on groceries, restaurants, and other expenses.

Slowly, we stocked up our emergency fund. One hundred dollars one month, five hundred dollars another. Dollar by dollar, we built it up to three months' worth of expenses. And then, over time, we continued to increase it until we got to six months' worth of expense.

Building an emergency fund is a long-term process made up of small, intentional actions.

I recommend working toward having three to six months of expenses set aside in a savings account. If you have zero saved today, work toward that long-term goal, but don't over-focus on it. Instead, put your primary focus on short-term goals, like putting money into your emergency fund regularly. Fifty dollars here and one hundred dollars there adds up over time.

An emergency fund is important, especially for those with student loans. People who have student loan debt are more likely to feel trapped in their current life and work than others. Those who have no student loan or other debt typically have a different mindset than the millions who feel the burden of student loans.

Those with debt and no emergency fund to fall back on are vulnerable. They may feel a need to stay in their current job, even if it's a bad situation. They are more likely to lay low at work instead of speaking up. And we all know—or can imagine—that it's a lot more stressful constantly having that debt in the back of your mind.

---

41   We'll discuss side hustles in more detail starting on page 199.

You need an F off Fund

The phrase "F off Fund," or FoF, may sound a bit harsh to you, but the underlying concept is something important: empowerment. Paulette Perhach, author of *Welcome to the Writer's Life*, describes it this way:

"A FoF is enough money to tell anyone who deserves to be told to f off to indeed do so. It's the money you need to keep creepy or abusive people out of your life. Sadly, many of these people do an Academy Award-level job of acting nice or normal, until they realize they have power over you. If you have a FoF, you have more power over your own life, more autonomy to choose your circumstances, and more ability to say bye, or worse, to whomever you choose."

My fellow passive-aggressive Minnesotans' jaws may drop at such bluntness, but for many this is exactly what they need to hear. If you have student loan debt, especially if you have a lot of it, you are more likely to feel like you have fewer options because of it. It may make you feel the need to stay in a compromising—or even abusive—situation. This goes beyond student loans, though, and extends to anyone who does not have money set aside in an emergency fund. What an emergency fund represents is what Perhach described: the resources to not compromise. To have options. To not feel the need to be silent if you think something is wrong. To take money out of the equation and not think "What the hell will I do if I lose my job over this?"

I think many people will become much more excited about building an emergency fund if they think of it in terms of a FoF fund. It's not just about setting aside money in case your dog swallows a bone; it's about not letting others have power over you!

Perhach proposes a simple exercise to help you determine how much your FoF should be. She suggests making a list of everyone who has control over your resources. "It might be your boss who has control over your paycheck, your girlfriend who pays most of your rent, or your dad, whose insurance plan you're using. The next step is to calculate how much money you would need if you had to kick that person out of your life. Whatever the maximum amount is, that should be your goal FoF."

Next time you are struggling to find the motivation to save money in your emergency fund (after all, a trip to someplace warm in the middle of the winter sounds so much more appealing than letting money sit in a bank account), remind yourself that what you are building is a FoF.

Always pay the minimum on your student loans but, for the sake of your mental and financial health, I highly recommend building a solid emergency fund before making any extra payments toward your student loans.

Having twenty thousand dollars in an emergency fund and forty thousand dollars of student loan debt is better than having nothing in an emergency fund and twenty thousand dollars of student loan debt.

Whether you have an established emergency fund or not is a key piece of information when it comes to crafting your student loan strategy.

You may have heard highly regarded finance gurus recommend one thousand dollars as a target amount for an emergency fund, and once you hit one thousand dollars, you should focus on repaying debt. I think this is way too low, especially for people who have significant debt. The odds of having to go into credit card debt or take out personal loans are pretty high if your emergency fund stops at one thousand dollars. Three months is the minimum you should work toward, though having four, five, or six months' worth of expenses in an emergency fund is beneficial.

Medical Emergency Funds

Establishing a basic emergency fund should always be your top priority, and I don't want to distract from that, but I've found that having a separate medical emergency fund is becoming important in the United States. This may not seem like priority for you now, but it's worth considering because of the peace of mind and tax advantages that come with it.

High Deductible Health Plans (HDHPs) are here to stay, with more employers shifting toward offering *only* HDHPs. Many options in the health insurance exchanges are HDHPs. With a HDHP, there is typically as much as six thousand dollars you have to pay before your insurance coverage kicks in and starts covering costs. High out-of-pocket maximums, sometimes as high as the mid-teens, are becoming common.

While lower monthly premiums are one of the positives of HDHPs, there's no denying the fact that they have a dark side: unexpected health bills that many do not have the funds to cover. Four in ten adults either could not cover a four-hundred-dollar unexpected expense or could only cover it by selling something or borrowing money.[42]

---

42   "Report on the Economic Well-Being of U.S. Households in 2017," *The Federal Reserve*, https://www.federalreserve.gov/publications/files/2017-report-economic-well-being-us-households-201805.pdf. May 2018.

With this shift in mind, we need to prepare ourselves. We need to build a medical emergency fund. And we do this through a Health Savings Account (HSA).

HDHPs come with an HSA. The US government allows you to contribute up to a certain amount to your HSA, tax-free. For individuals, this is currently about $3,500 and, for couples or families, it's around $7,000.[43]

If you use the funds for qualified medical expenses,[44] you can take money out of your HSA tax-free. Tax-free in, tax-free out. Once you start using an HSA to pay qualified medical expenses, you will wonder why you haven't always taken advantage of this tax benefit.

One thing most people don't realize is that HSAs have an investment component as well. Once your HSA hits a certain threshold, say two thousand dollars, anything beyond that threshold can be moved to the investment portion of the HSA. Within this investment portion, there are mutual funds you can invest in.

This is huge, because you will not be taxed on the gains these investments make as long as you withdraw the funds to pay for a qualified medical expense. This is commonly referred to as the HSA "triple tax advantage":

- Put the funds in pre-tax

- Investment gains are not taxed

- Take the funds out without being taxed

That's some serious savings!

---

43 Check the IRS website for the most current information: https://www.irs.gov/

44 Check IRS Publication 502, Medical and Dental Expenses, for more info. In general, prescriptions and payments to medical providers fall under qualified medical expenses.

You may be wondering "What if my HSA grows and I have a huge account at retirement, but few medical issues?" First of all, that's a great problem to have. Second, you can withdraw money from an HSA for non-medical costs once you hit sixty-five and it will be taxed similarly to other tax-advantaged retirement accounts (i.e. a 401(k) or IRA). Note that if you withdraw for non-qualified medical costs prior to sixty-five, you will be hit with taxes *plus* a 20 percent penalty.

Finally, your employer may have an HSA match policy up to a certain dollar amount. If your employer offers this, don't pass up this "free" money.

Consider the fact that the average sixty-five-year old couple today can expect to spend $245,000 on healthcare costs in retirement,[45] not counting long-term care costs. Needless to say, the sooner you can start saving money in an HSA, the better.

Student Loans Aren't the Only Debt

I've read thousands of personal finance blog posts over the years, and one thing that has frustrated me at times is the lack of attention student loans receive. That's changed a bit recently, as the number of people with student loans and the average amount of student loan debt has risen.

More recently, I've been disappointed with the lack of coverage and attention that credit card and other debt has received. Despite student loan debt surpassing credit card debt, there are

---

45   "Health Care Costs for Couples in Retirement Rise to an Estimated $245,000," *Fidelity*, https://www.fidelity.com/about-fidelity/employer-services/health-care-costs-for-couples-retirement-rise. October 2015.

still many who struggle with it. It can be even more debilitating than student loans because of how high the interest rate is.

While credit card debt has one advantage over student loan debt because it can be discharged in bankruptcy,[46] bankruptcy is something that should be avoided whenever possible. Credit card debt often has much higher interest rates, typically more than 20 percent, so paying it off should be a top priority.

Some actions you should consider taking if you are in credit card debt:

- **Apply for a 0 Percent APR Transfer Credit Card**
  There are a number of credit cards out there that allow you to transfer your balance and pay no interest on it for a period of time, typically twelve or more months. This is a good option if you can fully pay off the balance in the period of time. For example, if you transfer $5,000 of credit card debt to a 0 percent APR card, you will want to make sure you can afford approximately $417/month in payments.

  Many charge a one-time fee when you make the transfer. You will also want to understand how interest is treated once the 0 percent term is up. Make sure you understand all the terms and conditions before you apply for the card and make the transfer, and do not take on any additional credit card debt.

- **Talk to a Credit Counselor**
  If you feel like you are drowning in debt and aren't sure how you are going to pay it off, don't hesitate to reach out to a credit counselor. The National Foundation for Credit

---

46   Student loan debt technically can be discharged in bankruptcy, but it's extremely difficult and rare.

Counseling is a nonprofit organization that provides access to credit counseling services. If you are struggling, this is something you should absolutely consider doing.

- **Refinance your Debt**
  Another option to lower the cost of your debt is through refinancing. There are a variety of lenders who offer personal loans at a (relatively) low interest rate that can be used to pay off credit card debt. For some, this works well, as they can finally start making progress on the principal of their debt.

- **Talk to Your Credit Card company**
  If you are struggling with your credit card debt, it can't hurt to talk to your credit card company. The worst-case scenario is that they will not offer you any relief. Ultimately, they don't want to see your balance go to collections, though. At that point, they can only hope to see a fraction of your debt make its way back to them, so they have incentive to provide you some form of relief.

- **Switch to Income-Driven Repayment (IDR) for Student Loans**
  It's difficult to pay off credit card debt if you are paying a large percentage of your income toward student loan debt. Move to an IDR plan and focus on getting rid of your higher-interest debt first.

Credit card debt can be daunting, but there are solutions. Keep making your monthly student loan payments while you pay off your credit card debt, but focus on eliminating credit card debt before making any additional payments to your student loans.

When Credit Card Debt Is Overwhelming

Because of how important credit card debt is, I spoke with an expert to get some additional insights on how best to go about paying it down and what the signs are that you need help from a professional. Leslie Tayne is the author of *Life & Debt* and founder of Tayne Law Group, PC. She's helped many who have been deep in debt. Here are some of her thoughts on a couple of important questions.

At what point should someone look for help with their credit card debt?

There are a few signs. One is when you realize that you are making minimum payments and not getting anywhere. When you have limited to no cash flow, meaning you carry no cash with you and wait for more money to come in to pay for things. Living paycheck-to-paycheck not only is strenuous on daily expenses, but it also puts your future at risk, and you cannot build savings.

If you are coming up short each month for your bills and are constantly worried about small expenses. "Forgetting to pay the bills" is a tell-tale sign that you may be struggling with a severe debt problem.

If someone is consistently relying on credit cards to pay for everything from groceries to monthly utility bills, even paying other credit cards off, this should signal it's time to get debt help. Credit card reliance is a perilous path financially, and the amount of debt will rapidly increase.

How can someone tell if the debt counselor or lawyer they are working with is legitimate and not a scam? How do they know if they are getting a good arrangement that will help them get out of debt?

I first tell everyone to go with your gut. If it doesn't feel right, then it probably isn't, and you should just move on. Reputation and time in the industry are important.

You're interviewing someone to do an important job for you, so make sure you ask questions and do some research. Good questions to ask include:

- How long have they been in business?

- Is this their primary business?

- Are they really a bankruptcy attorney who says they do debt settlement (which is common)?

- Do they want money up front?

- Can you meet with them?

- Who is doing the negotiations and handling your money?

- What happens if you're sued?

I've heard the "attorney on staff" line so many times, but does that mean that attorney is *your* attorney? You can probably guess that person is not your personal attorney. If you're looking to get rid of the burden of your debt, the last thing you want to be dealing with is a scam from a company that promises to help.

The best arrangement is one where expectations are managed. You can't afford to go into one of these scenarios with unrealistic expectations, and that's another way to know if you're dealing with the right people. Are they managing your expectations from the beginning? Or are they just telling you "Don't worry, we do this and that and will save you lots of money" and tons of one-liners?

It's not all about saving you money; it's about a resolution to a more significant financial issue that strategically needs to be done right. The company you are working with should treat you as an individual, know your short- and long-term goals, and be able to lay out a clear road to recovery.

Other Debt

Credit card debt is the most immediate concern, but what if you have other debt, such as a car or personal loan? If you have other debt besides student loans and credit card debt, I encourage you to focus on the interest rate on the debt.

If you have a personal loan at, say, 10 percent, it's a relatively high rate and should be prioritized ahead of lower-interest debt (such as student loans). On the flip side, if you have a mortgage or an auto loan at a low rate like 4 percent, I recommend first focusing on other higher-interest debt, and even considering investing for retirement before making additional payments.

By this point, you should already have a spreadsheet with your student loan debt details. If you have other debt, use the other debt-tracking tab within your spreadsheet[47] and populate it with the type of debt, interest rate, minimum monthly payment, balance, and any other relevant information.

Once you have this laid out, take a step back and think about your debt. Is it high-interest? Low-interest? How far behind are you on payments, if at all?

_____

_____

_____

_____

_____

---

47   If you used the spreadsheet at StudentLoanSolutionBook.com, there is a tab set up for this exercise.

In what order should you tackle your debt? And what actions can you take (speaking to a credit counselor, refinancing, etc.) to better deal with your debt?

_____

_____

_____

_____

_____

- -

If you have debt other than student loans, it's important to factor that into your student loan strategy. Especially if you have higher-interest debt, you will want to eliminate this debt before putting anything additional toward your student loans.

Investing

A question many people struggle with is whether to invest or pay down debt.

We've all heard at one time or another, "The earlier you start investing, the more money you will have in retirement." Easier said than done, especially if you are one of the millions struggling with crippling student loan debt.

You likely fall into one of these three categories:

- **You haven't started investing for retirement.**
- **You invest a little, but not much.**

- **You are making minimum payments on debt and investing as much as possible of what's left over.**

Considering the psychological impact of student loans, I'm never surprised when I hear someone say they are focused on their debt, leaving investing on the back burner. Those who pay the minimum on their debt and invest what's left over are likely the outliers.

One of the risks of investing is the economy tanking, wiping out gains. It took years for the stock market to bounce back after the recession that started in 2008. In the years leading up to the recession, you would have been better off focusing on paying down debt than exposing more and more of your money to the market.

On the flip side, those who haven't been investing since the market dropped have missed out on a huge bull market. Some stocks have consistently gained 20 percent or more a year on average. Paying down debt that's at 3, 4, 7, or even 10 percent meant missing out on some significant gains that could have then compounded for the next twenty, thirty, or more years.

The one problem with everything I just said is that it's backward-looking. Of course, if you knew how the market was going to move, you'd make the exact right investments and money moves. Trying to predict where the market is going, or in other words "timing the market," is exactly what you should avoid when you are investing. Investing should be a consistent, long-term strategy.

Let's talk about a couple things that we do know for certain that make sense for you to take advantage of, and then let's figure out at what interest rate you should consider investing instead of paying down debt.

Employer Retirement Match Is a Must

If your employer offers to match your contribution to a retirement account, such as a 401(k) or 403(b), you should take advantage of it. Besides paying the minimum required amount on your debt and building an emergency fund, contributing enough to your retirement account to max out the employer match should be a top priority.

Not taking advantage of a 100 percent or 50 percent match on your retirement contributions is like leaving money on the table. Think of it as one of the easiest ways to make extra money.

For example, your employer may have a 401(k) retirement plan where they match your contributions dollar for dollar for the first 3 percent of your salary you contribute, and then half of the next 3 percent (i.e. fifty cents for each dollar). Not every employer offers this, but, if your employer does, you should contribute enough to take full advantage of the match.

Employee Stock Purchase Program

A similar but less common employer perk is an employee stock purchase program, or ESPP. If your employer doesn't have stock, this won't be an option, but large corporations typically have some variation of an ESPP for employees to take advantage of.

One variation of an ESPP works like this. Before every six-month period, you can contribute up to 10 percent of your paycheck toward the ESPP. Each paycheck will automatically take out 10 percent, or whatever percentage you chose, and put it in a brokerage account. At the end of the six months, company stock will be purchased using these contributions. The stock isn't purchased at the market rate, though. Instead, the price at the beginning and the end of the six-month period are compared. The lower of the two is taken, and the money that was set aside throughout the six-month period will be used to purchase stock at that price...but at a 15 percent discount.

You are essentially guaranteed a 15 percent gain every six months. But that's only if the stock price decreases. Let's say the price went from $150 to $200 over the course of the six months. You will get stock at $150 x 85 percent, or $127.50. You could sell those shares immediately for a $72.50 (or 36 percent) gain per share. You can also hold the stock for a longer period of time to avoid short-term capital gains tax, and possibly see further gains.

If your employer offers you opportunities like this, take advantage of them. It's an easy way to "make" money, and your employer factors this into your compensation, whether you take advantage of it or not.

Debt Paydown Is Guaranteed

Investing comes with inherent risk. Over the long term, it's relatively safe to assume that your money will have average annual gains of around 8 percent, though historical performance doesn't guarantee future performance. But, in the short term, you could lose money, and, if you invest in individual stocks, there is always the risk that the company's stock could significantly lose value or the company could even go bankrupt and cease to exist.

With that in mind, paying off debt is guaranteed. It's guaranteed because you know if you pay a dollar of your debt, your debt decreases by a dollar.[48] The same can't be said about a dollar

---

48   If you do make extra payments toward your debt, make sure your loan servicer knows
     that you want the extra payment to go toward the principal.

in the stock market. Over the next year, it could increase by 10 percent, double in price, drop 20 percent, or any other range of possibilities. There are no guarantees. Paying down debt is the more conservative option because you know the end result.

There is also a psychological aspect of debt that can't be ignored. For some, there is a huge difference between having zero debt and a zero net worth compared to having one hundred thousand dollars in investments and one hundred thousand dollars of debt. The interest rate doesn't matter to them; all that matters is that they owe someone money, and it will be on their mind until the debt is gone.

Erin Lowry, author of *Broke Millennial Takes on Investing: A Beginner's Guide to Leveling-Up Your Money*, agrees that psychology plays a part in whether someone should invest while holding student loan debt. "Sure, having debt at 3 percent interest may mean it makes more sense to invest as well instead of throwing all your spare money toward debt freedom. But if you can't sleep at night knowing this debt is looming over you and it causes you a lot of angst, screw it and pay off the debt. However, I still think you should at least take advantage of an employer-match on retirement."

So When Should You Invest? When Should You Pay Down Debt?

If you want to be more aggressive, you may wonder at what interest rate you should invest instead of paying down debt. Is it 8 percent? More? Less? How much more or less? Assuming you want to take the optimal approach and are not stuck on taking the conservative approach of paying down debt instead of investing, we need a threshold to help us determine this.

Lowry looked into this very question when writing her book. "I asked a lot of professionals: When does it make sense to invest while carrying student loan debt, and when should you focus on your debt? Without fail, every single person I asked recommended at least getting the match on an employer-sponsored retirement plan, and then focus on paying off anything at or above a 5 percent interest rate. The logic being you won't necessarily get the better return investing that money as you will with the guaranteed return of paying off the debt."

This 5 percent figure is cited frequently by experts and is a good benchmark to go by. One reason why the benchmark is 5 percent and not higher (after all, we rarely hear experts say the stock market returns only 5 percent annually) is that gains are taxed. Ultimately, the average pre-tax return of the stock market isn't a perfect benchmark. Paying down debt has the added advantage of being guaranteed. You may miss out on a bull market where investments are increasing much faster than normal, but you also may miss out on a bear market where investments are losing value or stagnating.

At the end of the day, you need to decide what approach you are most comfortable with.

Key Takeaways

- Review the past three months of income and expenses and determine your cash flow, noting how positive or negative it is.

- An emergency fund should be prioritized over making extra payments toward debt and is an essential safety net for someone who is in debt.

- Credit card and other high-interest debt should be prioritized over student loan debt. If you are struggling with credit card debt, talk to a credit counselor.

- Take advantage of a 401(k) match, 403(b) match, ESPP, and HSA match before paying extra toward debt.

- Debt paydown is guaranteed, while future stock market returns are not and can vary, especially in the short term.

- If your debt is at an interest rate of 5 percent or lower, consider investing before making extra payments toward your debt.

Step 4:

Decision Time–Choose Your Repayment Strategy

You've done all the prep work. Now it's time to bring everything together and choose a repayment strategy that works for you.

Remember: Everyone has a unique situation!

Your situation may be similar to others', but no situation is exactly the same as yours. This should drive *all* your financial decisions—not just what student loan repayment plan to use. When you hear financial advice, always ask yourself, "How does this apply to my situation? *Does* it apply to me?"

Keep that in mind as you go through this step. Ultimately, your repayment strategy should be what works for you.

Bring It All Together

As we've gone through the first three steps, you've gained a bunch of useful information about your loans and your finances. This up-front work will pay off in the end.

As a reminder, here are the things you should know at this point:

Steps #1 and #2: Loans and Options

- What type(s) of student loans do you have?

- How much do you have in student loans? How much of each type of student loan?

- What's the interest rate on your student loans?

- What income-driven repayment (IDR) plans are you eligible for?

- How does your monthly payment compare on the standard ten-year repayment plan versus the IDR plans?

- If you are in default or behind on your payments, what are the next steps you need to take to get your loans current?

- Based on your employer, are you eligible for loan forgiveness through Public Service Loan Forgiveness?

Step #3: Your Financial Situation

- What does your cash flow look like? How much extra money do you have coming in each month?

- Do you have an emergency fund? If so, how many months of expenses would it cover if you suddenly became unemployed? If not, what steps do you need to take to build an emergency fund?

- What other debt do you have besides student loans?

- What's the interest rate on your non-student loan debt?

- If it's available to you, are you taking advantage of 401(k) match, 403(b) match, ESPP, and/or HSA match?

If you don't already know the answers to these questions, work through them one by one.

I am sympathetic to the mindset that all debt is bad and getting rid of debt as quickly as possible will lead to a healthier and more fulfilling life. Debt can affect our emotions like few other things can. That's why some people do things like pay off their mortgage as quickly as possible despite having a low interest rate.

There are many who would benefit greatly from an IDR plan, because their current income makes the standard ten-year repayment plan unaffordable. In these situations, it's better to move to an IDR plan than to risk defaulting on student loans. Moving to an IDR plan and focusing on other financial priorities, like saving and investing, is particularly attractive for those who are pursuing a career that would make them eligible for PSLF.

How do you actually know what your repayment plan should be? For example, do you know how much in monthly payments it would take for you to pay off your loans in three years? Five years?

Let's go over a couple of examples, as well as run your numbers so you have the information necessary to choose the best payoff timeline.

Example of the Impact of Different Repayment Timelines

In this example, let's assume you have $45,000 of student loan debt with a weighted average interest rate of 6.5 percent.

Based on these numbers, to pay off your loans in one year, you would have to make monthly payments of $3,883, which equate to $46,600 a year. Alternatively, to pay these loans off in five years you would need to make monthly payments of $880, which translates to approximately $10,500 a year.

Years to Repayment	Monthly Payment	Annual Payment
1	$ 3,883	$ 46,600
2	$ 2,005	$ 24,055
3	$ 1,379	$ 16,550
4	$ 1,067	$ 12,806
5	$ 880	$ 10,566
6	$ 756	$ 9,077
7	$ 668	$ 8,019
8	$ 602	$ 7,229
9	$ 551	$ 6,617
10	$ 511	$ 6,132

For most, the forty-seven thousand dollars you would need to pay off your loans in one year is beyond unrealistic. It's an outrageous amount.

But perhaps the lower monthly payments required to pay off the loans in five to ten years are realistic. If you can afford an extra $370 a month on top of the required $511 monthly payment on the standard ten-year repayment plan, you can shave five (!) years off your repayment plan.

Perhaps you have a specific target in mind. If you are, say, twenty-six years old and you want to have your loans eliminated by the time you are thirty, you may want to see what monthly payments you would have to make to accomplish this goal.

Let's say your thirtieth birthday is forty-four months away. The numbers play out like this:

Desired Months	44
Years to Repayment	3.7
Monthly Payment	$1,152
Annual Payment	$13,826

To knock out your loans by your birthday, you would need to make approximately $1,150 monthly payments for the next forty-four months.

Plug your student loans into the aggressive repayment calculator within the student loan spreadsheet available at StudentLoanSolutionBook.com and see what aggressive repayment would look like for you.

Let's look at another scenario. Below is $100,000 in debt at a weighted average interest rate of 6.5 percent.

Years to Repayment	Monthly Payment	Annual Payment
1	$ 8,630	$ 103,556
2	$ 4,455	$ 53,456
3	$ 3,065	$ 36,779
4	$ 2,371	$ 28,458
5	$ 1,957	$ 23,479
6	$ 1,681	$ 20,172
7	$ 1,485	$ 17,819
8	$ 1,339	$ 16,063
9	$ 1,225	$ 14,705
10	$ 1,135	$ 13,626

With this amount of debt, the minimum required monthly payment on a standard ten-year repayment plan is $1,135 a month. For many who are just out of college, this is a lot of money. To pay this amount of debt off in three years, you would need to contribute $37,000 annually toward your student loans.

To put this in perspective, let's say you make $35,000 a year out of college and have $100,000 of debt. Even if you made $35,000 *after* taxes and contributed every last dollar toward your student loans, you literally would not make enough to knock out your debt in three years. You also might have a tough time even coming up with the $1,135 a month required for the standard ten-year repayment plan.

If you are in a situation where the required monthly payment looks difficult or impossible, the aggressive repayment options simply aren't going to work for you unless you make some changes. It's not impossible to aggressively pay down your debt even when the ten-year repayment looks daunting, but it does take significant sacrifice. You would need to drastically cut expenses and/or find a way to significantly increase your income.

In these situations, I recommend moving to an IDR plan and exploring whether Public Service Loan Forgiveness is an option for you. That way, you will have reasonable monthly payments that will allow you to build an emergency fund, start saving for retirement, and get yourself in a good place financially. If your financial situation changes down the road, you can always reevaluate your situation and see if aggressively paying down your loans makes sense.

Which Strategy Fits You?

Armed with a wealth of information (no pun intended) on your loans and financial situation, let's take a look at five different repayment strategies and see which best fits your situation.

Strategy #1: Pay Off Your Loans Faster Than the Standard Ten-Year Repayment Plan

This strategy is relatively straightforward: Eliminate your student loans quickly. It involves making extra payments toward your student loan debt that help eliminate your debt faster than if you made minimum payments on a standard ten-year repayment plan.

This is the best strategy for: Those who are in a financial situation, including having the necessary income, to make extra payments toward their student loan debt.

Before paying extra toward your student loans, you should have done the following:

- Built an emergency fund that is at a minimum equivalent to three months of expenses.

- Eliminated high-interest debt.

- Maxed out your employer's 401(k) match, 403(b) match, ESPP, and/or HSA match.

If your goal is to pay off your student loans as quickly as possible, you are in good company. There are many who have taken this approach and paid off their loans in less than ten years through discipline, side hustles, and making every decision based on whether it will help them pay off their student loans ASAP.

Paying Down Debt Faster

If part of your plan is to pay off your debt aggressively, there are two popular approaches you can take: the debt avalanche or the debt snowball.

Debt Avalanche

The debt avalanche is a strategy for paying down debt where you pay the minimum on all your loans and put any extra money toward the loan with the highest interest rate. This approach makes the most sense mathematically because the loans with the highest interest rates are costing you more than the loans with lower interest rates.

Say you have the five student loans listed below.

Loan Amount	Interest Rate
$5,000	4.8 percent
$20,000	6.0 percent

$2,000	3.2 percent
$10,000	4.2 percent
$7,000	5.0 percent

Using the debt avalanche you would pay the minimum on all the loans and put any extra funds, say $200 a month, toward the $20,000 loan at 6.0 percent.

Once you pay off the $20,000 loan, you would put the extra $200 toward the $7,000 loan at 5.0 percent. You'd also put in whatever the minimum monthly payment was for the $20,000 loan. Let's say it was $500 a month. You'd now not only be paying the minimum required monthly payment on the $7,000 loan, but also an additional $700 a month (the original $200 a month extra you were putting toward the $20,000 loan, plus the $500 minimum payment you were making toward the $20,000 loan). You'd continue this process until all your loans were eliminated.

Debt Snowball

The debt snowball is similar to the debt avalanche in the sense that you make the minimum payments on your loans and put any extra money toward a specific loan. It differs, though, because interest rate is not a factor—size of the loan is.

Loan Amount	Interest Rate
$5,000	4.8 percent
$20,000	6.0 percent
$2,000	3.2 percent
$10,000	4.2 percent
$7,000	5.0 percent

Looking at the same five loans, we would not start out by contributing any extra money toward our $20,000 loan. Instead, we would put funds toward the $2,000 loan. Once the $2,000 loan is gone, we would move on to the $5,000 loan, and so forth.

This approach plays to our emotions. You will eliminate the $2,000 loan much faster using the debt snowball approach than you would eliminate the $20,000 loan using the debt avalanche approach, simply due to the sheer difference in size of the loans. Getting small wins early on can keep you motivated to stick with the plan and continue to attack your debt. It's a definite possibility that you will lose motivation with the debt avalanche and abandon the plan before fully eliminating your debt.

So which approach is better? It depends. If you have a few small loans and a few large loans, it may make sense to take the debt snowball approach to get some quick wins. On the flip side, if all your loans are similar in size or you have some loans with much higher interest rates and some with low interest rates, the debt avalanche may make more sense.

I've spent years working in both corporate and personal finance, so the finance and math person in me can't help but advocate for the debt avalanche over the debt snowball. Logically, it *does* make sense. My years in personal finance have also taught me something else, though: money is usually emotional. Which is why the debt snowball is sometimes, if not often, preferred.

Psychology comes into play with money more than most would like to think. Do what works for you, and be honest with yourself about which approach you are more likely to stick with.

In What Order Should I Pay Off My Student Loans?

Not all student loans are created equal, so it may not always make sense to focus solely on interest rate.

If you have a variety of student loans, my recommended order of paydown would be:

1. Private Student Loans

2. Federal Unsubsidized Loans

3. Federal Subsidized Loans

Of all student loans, private student loans are the least favorable, and federal subsidized loans are the most favorable. Remember that federal subsidized loans do not accrue interest while in deferment and have some form of interest benefit for income-driven repayment (IDR) plans (except for the Income-Contingent Repayment plan).

If you go with the strategy of paying off your loans as fast as you can, ask yourself the following questions:

Do a full audit of your income and expenses. Can you make more? Spend less? Both? What other finance hacks can you take advantage of to increase cash flow (see tips in step five)?

_____

_____

_____

Are there other financial priorities, like building an emergency fund or investing for retirement, that should be focused on instead of putting extra cash flow to student loans?

_____

_____

_____

How much extra money can you realistically put toward your loans?

_____

_____

_____

Once you know how much extra you can put toward your loans, figure out what that translates to in a timeline. Use a target payoff date as motivation to stick to your plan.

My target payoff date is: _____

Does it make sense to refinance to save on interest? Refer back to page 54, where we went over refinancing. If you are able to get a lower interest rate through refinancing, it could speed up your target payoff date.

Strategy #2: Standard Ten-Year Repayment Plan

This strategy involves making minimum monthly payments on the standard ten-year repayment plan and using any additional cash flow to improve other areas of your finances.

This is the best strategy for: Those who can afford the standard ten-year repayment plan, would prefer to work toward other financial goals, and are comfortable paying their student loans for ten years.

If you want to pursue this strategy, you should be able to afford the monthly minimum payment on the standard ten-year repayment plan while also having cash flow left over to build an emergency fund, pay off high-interest debt, and/or pursue other financial goals, like saving for a home or investing. If this isn't the case, you need to move to an IDR plan, increase your income through your nine-to-five or side hustle, and/or reduce your expenses

This is the ideal plan because it has a definitive end date, but there are people who stay on the standard ten-year repayment plan who end up struggling and falling behind. If the standard ten-year repayment plan is stretching you too far, you risk falling behind and defaulting on your loans, which ultimately will cause you to pay more due to interest and fees.

Things you should be working toward while paying the minimum on your student loans include:

- Building a three-month (or longer) emergency fund.

- Eliminating high-interest debt.

- Maxing out tax-advantaged retirement accounts such as a 401(k), 403(b), and/or IRA.

- Maxing out your HSA contributions.

- Saving for a down payment on a home (if this is important to you).

Refinance Student Loans?

If you only have private student loans or have refinanced your student loans once already, there is no risk in exploring refinance opportunities with other lenders, which could potentially save you money. On the flip side, refinancing federal student loans can be risky. By refinancing with a private lender, you are giving up the option of IDR, the possibility of loan forgiveness, and other favorable terms such as interest benefits that come with subsidized federal loans. It can't be undone.

You may be in a unique situation, though, where refinancing your federal student loans makes sense if you are…

- on the standard ten-year repayment plan *and*

- can afford to pay more toward your student loans *and*

- are choosing to continue paying the minimum while pursuing other financial goals

Sure, there are risks that come with refinancing, but, if you can knock your interest rate down to a favorable percentage, you could save thousands on interest that can be diverted toward your other financial goals. It becomes even more attractive when you consider the longer timeline on which you will be paying down your debt (ten years as opposed to aggressively paying it down in, say, one to five years). With that said, you should only refinance if you have built an emergency fund and have eliminated your high-interest debt.

Strategy #3: Get on an Income-Driven Repayment (IDR) Plan

This strategy involves enrolling in one of the four IDR plans (PAYE, REPAYE, IBR, or ICR) which cap your monthly payments at a percentage of your income.

This is the best strategy for: Those who would be contributing significantly more than 10 percent of their discretionary income toward their student loans under the standard ten-year repayment plan, and/or those who would find it difficult or impossible to build an emergency fund, pay down high-interest debt, and take advantage of employer perks like a 401(k)/403(b) match, HSA match, and/or ESPP.

IDR plans are the primary tool that borrowers should use to avoid falling behind and defaulting on their student loans. These plans can be a lifeline to borrowers who otherwise would be stuck making payments that eat up a majority of their income, causing them to inevitably default on their loans.

It may be difficult to know if you should switch off the standard ten-year repayment plan and move to an IDR plan. This is why we went through so much work before picking a repayment strategy. Refer back to some of the exercises you did and think about the following:

- How big is the difference in your projected payment under the standard ten-year repayment plan versus an IDR plan?

- Is it a material amount? Meaning, is it fifty dollars or five hundred dollars a month? If not, then sticking with the standard ten-year repayment plan may be best. If it is material, though, ask yourself a few more questions.

- Based on your income and expense tracking, what does your cash flow look like with each payment? If it's tight under the standard ten-year repayment plan, consider moving to an IDR plan. Remember, you can always switch back or make additional payments toward your debt.

- If an IDR plan frees up cash flow to build an emergency fund faster, pay off high-interest credit card debt faster, and take advantage of employer 401(k)/403(b) match and other employee perks, it is probably your best option. is recommended.

One thing worth pointing out is that switching to an IDR plan doesn't mean you will use the extra cash flow to improve your finances. You need to be disciplined and actually make the choice to save money, pay off debt, and make other smart money moves.

If you are given the opportunity to have reduced payments, don't waste it. Use the extra cash flow to make smart money moves!

Strategy #4: Pursue Public Service Loan Forgiveness

Pursuing Public Service Loan Forgiveness (PSLF) can be a huge financial win for those who are eligible. It takes strategy number three, getting on an IDR plan, and goes a step further.

This is the best strategy for: Those who work at a qualified employer and whose monthly payment would be less under an IDR plan than under a standard ten-year repayment plan.

If you work for a qualified employer and have a high amount of student loans, there's a good chance that PSLF makes sense. Of course, there is always the chance that your income is too high and your debt too low for this strategy to work (which is a good problem to have, by the way). In this case, you are better off sticking with the standard ten-year repayment plan or even aggressively paying off your debt.

Based on how expensive undergrad and grad school have become, and the relatively low wages that some nonprofit and government jobs pay, there are many who would benefit from switching to an IDR plan.

As mentioned earlier when we reviewed IDR plans, the monthly payment you make on these plans is based on your Adjusted Gross Income. Your AGI is calculated each year for tax purposes. There are ways to lower your AGI, which in turn would lower the amount you pay each month on your student loans, and ultimately increases the amount that is forgiven.

> **Adjusted Gross Income**: Gross income is how much money you make before taxes or deductions are taken out. Once you take out deductions, such as the standard deduction, you get a lower amount that is your AGI.

- **Contribute to a 401(k) or 403(b) Retirement Account**

  Pre-tax contributions to a 401(k) or 403(b) will reduce your AGI because it lowers your taxable income. These retirement accounts shield your income from taxes until you withdraw from them in retirement.

  If you are an employee, you can figure out details of your company's 401(k) and 403(b) by reaching out to your human resources department. They will either give directions on how to change your pre-tax contribution percentage online, or they will be able to adjust it for you.

  If you are self-employed, you will want to look into a solo 401(k). Many companies that offer IRAs also offer solo 401(k) options. It may be easier to look into a solo 401(k) after maxing out your IRA, which we discuss next.

- **Contribute to an IRA**

  Contributions to a standard IRA lower your AGI. Make sure you are contributing to a standard IRA, though, and not a Roth IRA. A Roth IRA is a retirement account that takes after-tax money and allows your contributions to gain value tax-free. A standard IRA is a retirement account that takes pre-tax money. You will be taxed when you take money out of this account during retirement. If your goal is to minimize your AGI and, in turn, maximize the amount you get forgiven via PSLF, a standard IRA is the way to go.

Many major brokerage companies that offer accounts for you to buy and sell stock also offer IRAs. Find a well-known company you are comfortable with and set up an IRA with them to start saving for retirement.

- **Contribute to a Health Savings Account**
  Contributing to a Health Savings Account, or HSA, lowers your taxable income. This also has the dual benefit of creating a medical emergency fund and an alternative retirement fund. Read more about HSAs on page 134.

Are you on an IDR plan like REPAYE that factors in your spouse's income? If so, remember that you can both make these financial moves. If your spouse is a high earner, you could technically both max out your contributions to lower the amount of income included in your AGI. Your paycheck may look tiny because so much is going to your retirement account, but that may be fine since you can live off your spouse's income. The name of the game is to make the allowed moves to lower your AGI, and in the process make smart money moves that set you up well for the future.

The only downside to these moves is that they lower the actual cash that you have for living expenses and discretionary spending. In my mind, if you are working toward PSLF, you are making short-term sacrifices to catapult yourself into a much better financial spot after 120 qualified monthly payments. If you weren't going to have any of your loans forgiven or were on a traditional path of loan forgiveness that can take twenty to twenty-five years, you'd have to sacrifice a lot longer or would not receive as big of a financial boost. While it may be challenging for the ten years you are making payments, PSLF can be a big win in the end.

I want to point out that in some situations it may hurt you long-term to switch to an employer solely for PSLF. For example, if you make sixty thousand dollars a year as a senior financial analyst at a private company, it may not make sense to switch to a similar government job that pays thirty-eight thousand dollars a year. The private company may have upside in the form of higher pay and career progression. Take a look at the pay differential and career development opportunities, and factor that together with your long-term career goals. For some, PSLF will be an easy choice; for others it may take some number crunching and reflection to decide if it's worth pursuing.

Strategy #5: Take Longer than Ten Years to Repay (with No Income-Driven Repayment Option)

Many borrowers today have some private student loans, and there are some who *only* have private student loans (i.e. if they refinanced with a private lender). But not everyone can afford the standard ten-year repayment plan that many private student loans typically default to. At the same time, private student loans do not have the same options for repayment as federal student loans. If you need to decrease your private loan payments, strategy five is for you.

This is the best strategy for: Those with private student loans who are struggling to afford the minimum monthly payment.

If only a portion of your student loans are private, make sure you prioritize paying those down first. If you've already refinanced, though, and have a relatively large amount of private student loans, you may find yourself in a situation where you simply can't afford the minimum monthly payment. If you find yourself in this situation, there are a couple of things you should consider doing:

- **Work with Your Current Lender**
  Call your lender and tell them about your situation. This may be the quickest and easiest way to get relief.

  If you are unemployed, they may have hardship options available, which mimic forbearance for federal student loans.

  If the issue is with your income relative to your debt, see if you can renegotiate your plan. If your monthly payment goes down in a renegotiated plan, you can expect that your timeline to repayment will increase (i.e. from ten to fifteen years).

- **See what other lenders are offering**
  There are a variety of banks that offer student loan refinance. It's becoming a big business with banks rolling out new refinance products. If your current lender isn't willing to renegotiate a more reasonable payment plan, it's worth seeing what other lenders may offer you. You can see a list of lenders at StudentLoanSolutionBook.com/Refinance.

With private loans, credit score and income come into play. It's similar to applying for any private loan, where having a higher credit score benefits you. Doing what you can to improve your credit history and credit score is worthwhile, not just for this, but also for other areas of your finances. Read more about improving your credit score on page 218.

Your interest rate will likely be more favorable if you have a cosigner, especially a cosigner with a good credit history. You may want to think twice about getting a cosigner for your private student loan refinance, though, for a morbid reason: there's a risk that, if you pass away before the loans are repaid, your cosigner will be stuck with the bill.

If you do extend your repayment term beyond ten years, I highly recommend you do what you can to improve your finances and pay extra toward your student loans. Private student loans do not offer forgiveness and you will need to pay them off eventually, so making repayment a priority in your life and shooting for ten years or less to full repayment is a worthwhile goal.

Hybrid Approach

You would think five different strategies would be enough, but you may be in a situation where your strategy benefits from a hybrid approach.

For example, let's say you have eighty thousand dollars in federal loans and twenty thousand dollars in private loans. Based on your income and financial situation, you move your federal loans onto an IDR plan. But what about your private student loans? You may want to take an approach where you pay them off ASAP.

When my wife and I started to repay our student loans, we took a similar approach to what I just described. We used strategy #2 for our federal and state student loans, which meant staying on the standard ten-year repayment plan while focusing on other financial goals. With our private student loans, though, we took the approach of paying them off as quickly as possible.

The moment you've been waiting for: pick your strategy and take the necessary actions to put it in motion!

Accountability–Stick to the Plan

Once you have a repayment strategy, you need to stick to the plan. That means staying disciplined and actually following through.

There are two specific things I recommend doing to stay accountable to your plan:

Automatic Payments

Automatic payments are a good way to stay on top of your loans and keep them current. On a broader scale, automating your finances is generally a good idea. I like to call it "automating good decisions." For example, you may put two hundred dollars in your emergency fund each month. Instead of having to make this decision month after month, set up automatic two-hundred-dollar monthly transfers from your checking to your savings account. By doing this, you don't have to even think about the decision—it will automatically happen each month!

If you haven't already, automate your minimum student loan payments. Then, automate other financial transactions, like bill payments and transfers from your checking to your savings account/ emergency fund.

Accountability Partner

You can have all the good intentions in the world but still not stick with your plan. Remember, you could be paying off student loans twice as long as you were in college, or even longer. It's a long-term plan. Having accountability will increase your chances of success.

An accountability partner can be a partner, friend, mentor, or really anyone who is going to make sure you stay on course with your repayment plan. If your accountability partner is your significant other and you are acting as a team in repaying your loans, it may be best for both of you to find a second accountability partner. Having an outside party keep you both on track can be beneficial.

Shannon McLay, the founder and CEO of The Financial Gym, shared these thoughts on the importance of accountability for those who are paying down student loans:

> Paying down student loans, no matter how much you have, typically takes multiple years; I imagine that it's like hiking Mt. Everest. You are not going to do it overnight; you are going to have to train for it, and it will involve a multi-step process. Most people do not climb or train to climb Everest alone for all of these reasons, and it's exactly why I think

you need accountability in your student loan repayment journey. There will be many times you want to quit. You'll get distracted or you'll just lose energy and get what I call "Debt Fatigued." In those moments, accountability is what takes you to the next level.

If you want to stay on track with your student loan repayment strategy, my recommendation is to get a financial trainer or money coach. Money coaching is a relatively new concept. You pay a flat fee or monthly subscription with a company or individual, and in return they meet with you regularly to discuss and review your financial goals, track your progress and, yes, keep you accountable. McLay's company, The Financial Gym, has financial trainers who have experience working with those who are repaying student loan debt. McLay says, "Financial trainers at the Gym work with clients of all shapes and sizes, and the plans vary based on the client's primary financial goals. For our clients paying down student loan debt, we take a balanced approach where we want to see them save for life goals while I also paying down the debt, instead of focusing entirely on debt repayment."

It may be difficult to imagine adding the cost of a money coach or financial trainer to your already stretched finances. My recommendation would be to cut back in other areas of your budget to make it feasible and give it a trial run. Additionally, you should think of it as an investment; you should expect your finances to improve when you work with a money coach or financial trainer.

It's worth mentioning that a more traditional way to go about financial planning is through a Certified Financial Planner or CFP. Individuals with the CFP certification have, among other things, passed the CFP exam, demonstrated financial planning experience, and agreed to uphold the fiduciary standard of care, which requires that a financial adviser act solely in the client's best interest when offering personalized financial advice. When you think of a CFP, you may think of someone who charges a certain percentage of your assets as an advisor's fee. You also may think "but I don't *have* any assets!" If this describes you, it may be worthwhile to reach out to a financial advisor and see if they are willing to work with you on a per-hour basis.

Find an accountability partner, whether it's a partner, family member, spouse, or financial trainer. Set up monthly or, at minimum, quarterly check-ins. Put these meetings on your calendar and keep them!

Key Takeaways

- Use information about your student loans and your current financial situation to choose the best repayment strategy for you.

- Before aggressively paying down your loans, make sure you have an adequate emergency fund, no high-interest debt, and are taking advantage of an employer match of 401(k), 403(b), HSA, and other employee benefits like an ESPP.

- Use the debt snowball or debt avalanche to pay down your debt faster.

- If you decide to stick to the standard ten-year repayment plan, make sure you are making smart money moves that will help you reach other financial goals.

- If you choose an IDR plan, use the lower monthly payment to improve other areas of your finances, like creating an emergency fund, eliminating high-interest debt, and saving money for retirement.

- If you are pursuing Public Service Loan Forgiveness, make sure you are taking advantage of tax-advantaged accounts, like a 403(b) and standard IRA, which lower your Adjusted Gross Income as well as help maximize the amount you will be forgiven.

- "Automate" good financial decisions. Set up automatic student loan payments with your lenders. Another example is setting up automatic transfers from your checking to savings account each month to build an emergency fund.

- Find an accountability partner who will help you stick to your plan. Put meetings on your calendar.

- Regularly review your repayment strategy and financial situation to determine whether your strategy still makes sense.

Step 5:

A Brighter Tomorrow—Optimize Your Money

I've always felt like I was behind or that I had to do more because of my student loans.

It may be because we naturally compare ourselves to others. I see coworkers and friends buying a home, taking an awesome vacation, or talking about being debt-free, and I think about how my student loans are holding me back. I feel like I have to do more to push my finances ahead.

Do you ever feel that way too? That your loans keep you from getting on track with your money and your life?

I've gotten better at focusing on my own situation and not letting other people's circumstances and perspectives impact me. But it's impossible to fully get away from it.

I don't want to spend time managing my money and improving my finances because "the Joneses" just got back from a month-long trip to Tahiti.

I want my dreams and goals for my life to be the reason I pursue better finances.

That's what step five is all about. This step continues on and doesn't have a definitive end point. Yes, there are specific things that you should cross off your list, such as starting a budget and finding and taking advantage of opportunities to increase your income, but you should always be looking for ways to improve your financial life. There's always more you can learn and do.

Remembering why you want to improve your situation is important. For me, I've known for a long time that I don't want to work in corporate forever. I have dreams of starting and growing businesses. I can do this on the side, but it's not sustainable, nor my goal, to take that approach forever. This dream has made me want to make smart money moves and continue to learn about and improve my financial life. What's your motivation? Always keep it at the forefront of your mind.

Some finance topics are dry. If you've made it this far, you've likely already spent hours learning about your student loans, your repayment options, and your current financial situation and deciding what student loan strategy makes the most sense for you. It's a lot to work through, and it can be tiring. If you don't keep your "why" and your motivation at the front of your mind, it's unlikely you will follow through on all the little, not-so-exciting things that push your money situation into a better place.

Stay positive and know that you have control over many aspects of your money and your future. Let's go over some of the practical things you can do to keep pushing your financial life in the right direction.

Start a Budget—Gain Control

Control over your money is the name of the game. And nothing gives you control like a budget.

In step three, we reviewed the past three months of your income and expenses. Tracking your income and expenses is a key first step in budgeting. Once you know how much money you spend on various budget categories, it's time to set a limit, or target, for each of those categories. The purpose of a budget is to keep you informed and accountable: informed about how much you are spending and accountable to your predetermined spending limits.

There are various ways to budget, but, whether it's in a spreadsheet or through an app, you need to decide what works best for you and run with it. Let's start by going over the popular cash budget.

Cash Budget

One of the most popular approaches to budgeting is the cash budget. This is typically done using an envelope system, which was popularized by Dave Ramsey. It's relatively simple:

- Get an envelope for each spending category like Restaurants and Groceries.

- At the beginning of each month, put cash into each envelope. For example, you may put three hundred dollars into your Groceries envelope.

- Use the envelopes throughout the month. Once an envelope runs out of cash, you are done spending for that month. If you budgeted fifty dollars for clothes for the month and spend all of it the first day, you cannot spend any more money on clothes until the envelope is replenished next month.

This approach works because it forces you to limit your spending. Once you've spent the cash, you are done!

There is one big problem with the cash envelope system: it's completely impractical in today's digital world.

Let's be honest: *who uses cash these days?* Nearly all of my bills are paid and purchases made with a credit or debit card. I rarely even write a check these days.

The cash envelope system *does* work well, though, based on many testimonials. So that raises the question: is there any way to make it work in our digital world?

It may sound like a lot of work, but one solution is tracking your expenses and updating a spreadsheet daily or weekly. Each time you update your spreadsheet, you can assign the expenses to your budget categories and deduct that amount from your budget. Once you have no money left for that category, you are done spending on that category for the month.

Making this a daily or weekly routine will not only keep you up to date on how much you have left for discretionary spending like groceries, clothes, and going out to eat, but will also help you feel more in control of your finances as a whole.

If you take this approach, it's ideal to use just one checking account, so that your transactions are all in one place, and just one credit card. Having more than one or two accounts to grab transactions from will make you less likely to stick with it.

> Track your cash transactions in a notepad on your phone and regularly transfer them to your budget spreadsheet, app, or pen and paper expense tracker. This also works well to track your gambling wins and losses. But no one who is financially savvy gambles, right? Right…

Spreadsheet Budget

In step three, when we tracked your income and expenses, I recommended inputting all your data into a spreadsheet. I may be a bit biased, since I've spent more than twenty hours a week in spreadsheets for the past eight years in my corporate finance and accounting jobs, but even an extremely simple spreadsheet can be useful for budgeting purposes.

I mentioned earlier that there is a free budget spreadsheet that you can use at StudentLoanSolutionBook.com. It has an automation tool built into it that will pull in data from your checking account, credit cards, and other accounts that transactions run through. Using a spreadsheet like this may be intimidating and confusing for people who haven't used them often. Even if that's the case, I don't think you should rule out tracking your information on a spreadsheet. Because of this, there are two different budget spreadsheets I created that you can use, a simple one and a more complex one.

My sister tried out my budget spreadsheet and didn't like it (thanks, Sis[49]). It was too confusing. She was looking for something simple. She used my spreadsheet, but instead of using the automated tool, she manually updates it every morning with any new transactions on her account or cash she spent the previous day. It's a process that works for her and keeps her disciplined.

Another option is to add up all your expenses by hand and put them into a printed-out budget template. I've included these templates, along with all the other free companion materials, at StudentLoanSolutionBook.com.

A typical monthly budget will have your budgeted amount for each category as well as how much you actually end up spending.

---

49   She also didn't read my blog the first four years it was published—rude!

Month	July		Year	2019

Net Income	$ 4,800	Budget Spend	$ 4,030
Expenses	$ 4,223	Actual Spend	$ 4,223
Net Inflow / (Outflow)	$ 578	Difference	$ (193)

Category	Budget	Actual	Difference
Auto Expenses	$ -	$ 25	$ (25)
Auto Insurance	$ 75	$ 75	$ -
Auto Loan	$ 300	$ 300	$ -
Cable & Internet	$ 125	$ 125	$ -
Cell Phone	$ 175	$ 175	$ -
Clothes	$ 50	$ 85	$ (35)
Donation/Charity	$ 100	$ 100	$ -
Entertainment	$ 100	$ 30	$ 70
Gas	$ 250	$ 270	$ (20)
Gifts	$ -	$ 50	$ (50)
Groceries	$ 500	$ 400	$ 100
Gym	$ 50	$ -	$ 50
Hair Cuts	$ 20	$ 20	$ -
Health/Medicine	$ 50	$ 125	$ (75)
Home	$ 100	$ 150	$ (50)
Insurance - Other	$ -	$ -	$ -
Mortgage	$ 1,100	$ 1,100	$ -
Pets	$ 10	$ 18	$ (8)
Restaurants/Drinks/Out to Eat	$ 100	$ 220	$ (120)
School	$ -	$ -	$ -
Student Loans	$ 500	$ 500	$ -
Toiletries	$ 25	$ 45	$ (20)
Travel	$ -	$ 200	$ (200)
Utilities	$ 100	$ 155	$ (55)
All Other	$ 300	$ 55	$ 245
Total Expense	**$ 4,030**	**$ 4,223**	**$ (193)**

At the beginning of each month you should populate the "budget" column. Either weekly or monthly, you should update with your actual spending and see how it compares to your budget.

Using an App for Budgeting

I've talked about using cash-based and spreadsheet-based budgeting, but you may be thinking, "Isn't there an app for that?" There is!

Not surprisingly, there are many apps out there to help you budget. You may have heard of some of the more popular ones like Mint, You Need a Budget, Mvelopes, and EveryDollar.

Peter Anderson, founder of *Bible Money Matters*, has used You
Need a Budget for several years now. "I use the desktop version
of their software which comes with an app, and they also have
a web-based version. It's unique in the way it allows you to
budget your money to specific categories, so when you enter
your transactions you can immediately see how much money you
have left to spend in that category and stop when you've reached
the limit."

Another personal finance blogger who uses an app for budgeting
is Jason Butler, founder of *The Butler Journal*. He uses Mint and
says, "You can see all of your financial info in one place including
credit card balances, student loan balances and investments. I
also like that you create goals in the app."

While I personally do not use budget apps, I know some who
swear by them. If an app sounds appealing to you, test out some
of the popular ones and pick one you like.

How Do I Actually Set My Budget?

You've tracked your expenses and picked a tool or software
to help you budget. You are probably wondering: How do
I know how much I should *actually* be spending on each
budget category?

A good starting point is looking at your current spending by
category. Some categories you don't have much leverage over.
For example, if you aren't going to be able to change the cost of
your rent or mortgage for at least six months or a couple of years;
in the short term, the cost is fixed. Other areas like groceries,
restaurants, or entertainment, you may be able to influence.

You may be happy with the amount you spend, but there are
likely areas where you are spending more than you'd like. In the

next section, "Strategies and Hacks to Save Money," we'll go over how to save money on specific budget categories.

While your current spending is a good starting point, I also want to walk you through a popular way to set a budget. The 50-30-20 budget is a good framework and guide as to how much money you should be spending on broad categories.

The 50-30-20 Budget

The 50-30-20 budget breaks down your take-home pay into three buckets:

- 50 percent Needs
- 30 percent Wants
- 20 percent Savings/Investing/Debt Repayment

Your take-home pay is your income after accounting for taxes. Many people have money deducted from their paycheck for health insurance premiums, retirement account contributions, and other adjustments prior to the actual net "paycheck amount" that hits your checking account. For the sake of working through the 50-30-20 budget, add back to the net any non-tax deductions. That's your true "take-home pay" that will be divided among the 50-30-20 buckets.

- **50 Percent Needs**
  This is any necessary spending each month, for things like housing, food, health care, minimum debt payments, etc. For those with student loans, I would put the minimum payment amount in this category. If you have credit card debt, this would include the minimum payment. Transportation to get to a job would fall into this category as well.

- **30 Percent Wants**
  Going out to eat with friends, a movie or concert ticket, and Netflix are things that fall in the "Wants" bucket. They improve your quality of life, but you don't *need* them.

- **20 Percent Savings/Investing/Debt Repayment**
  The remaining 20 percent is what you put toward retirement savings, emergency fund savings, and debt repayment above and beyond the minimum required monthly payment.

The 50-30-20 breakout is not a strict breakdown of how your income should be allocated. It's a framework to use as a starting point. It will vary depending on things like how high your take-home income is, what the cost of housing is for the city you live in, and what percentage of your income your minimum debt payments eat up.

The "Needs" and "Wants" buckets can be gray areas as well. Having a roof over your head is a need, but at least a part of the cost of having a downtown apartment in a trendy area would fall into the "Want" bucket. Transportation to work is another good example. If you have a fifty-mile round-trip commute to work, gas would fall into the "Need" bucket. But the cost of having a brand-new car instead of a used one that costs a third as much is at least partially a "Want."

A few things I would recommend keeping in mind as you put together your budget:

- **Know Your Priorities**—If a weekly dinner out with your partner is important to you and cutting it out would be painful, look for things you spend money on that you can cut or reduce that you care less about, like cable or some other subscription.

- **Think about Life with Reduced Debt**—The 50-30-20 budgeting method is a nice straightforward way to set a budget, but, if you have debt, you likely will not want to stop at 20 percent for the Savings/Investing/Debt Repayment bucket. Paying down your debt and building up your savings and investments will significantly improve your life.

How Often to Check Your Spending

Unless you are following the cash envelope method of budgeting, where you literally take cash out of an envelope until the cnvelope is empty for the month, you need to regularly check your spending throughout the month to see if you are staying on budget. But how often should you check your spending? After the month is over? Weekly? Daily?

If you are new to budgeting or haven't budgeted in a long time, I highly recommend checking your spending on a weekly basis. Put it on your calendar so you have time set aside. This is important! After you've been budgeting for a while, you can either keep the weekly updates or switch to monthly.

At the end of each month, review your total budget versus total spending. Did you go over budget? Under budget? What was the driver? Going category by category is important as well. Did you spend two hundred dollars more on groceries than expected? Why did that happen?

If you consistently are over budget, you need to look at whether your budget is realistic, as well as whether you are actually making the tough choices that keep you within it. Read the "Strategies and Hacks to Save Money" section for ideas on how to cut the amount you spend.

Budgeting isn't something you do once and then you're set. You need to continually review and adjust. Long-term, it will pay off.

Budget for Unexpected Expenses

There are unexpected expenses that come up, so make sure you budget for them. Depending on what sort of unexpected expenses you have, you may want to budget fifty dollars, one hundred dollars, or more toward this category (I call it the "Other" category in my budget). When you have months without unexpected costs, you should put the budgeted amount in a savings account or a checking account specifically for these expenses.

The amount you spend each month on categories like household goods can fluctuate greatly. For example, you could spend five hundred dollars on furniture and other household goods (a coffee pot, blankets, lamps, etc.) one month and then nothing the next month. Some months your budget will exceed your expenses. When this happens, you should set aside extra money for months in which expenses exceed your budget.

Just like life isn't always predictable, neither is spending. You can plan ahead, but sometimes things come up. Something will break or fall apart, and you will need to replace it, sometimes immediately. Random things happen. You can't plan specifically for every purchase, but you can set aside money knowing these costs happen.

Seven Unexpected Expenses to Plan For

The first summer my wife and I were in our house, the basement flooded. The following winter, the drain connecting our house to the city's sewer line collapsed.

We all face unexpected expenses. You can't predict everything. Most of us can reasonably assume our sewer line won't collapse (what a joke!).

Life throws you curveballs, and that's why I'm so big on emergency funds. Having those dollars set aside will make it easier to remain calm when something expensive breaks.

Besides having an emergency fund, it can also help to be mentally prepared for those costs that are going to come up. It's usually a matter of when, not if.

Medical Costs—Especially with high-deductible health plans becoming the norm, you are going to eventually get hit with a big, unexpected medical bill. Sock away some money in your Health Savings Account.

Pets—I'm begging you: If you have a pet or are planning on getting one, know that emergencies happen. We brought our cat to the animal ER because she had a tumor behind her eye that was causing it to fill with blood. Whether it's old age or your pet eating something they shouldn't have, bills in the thousands aren't impossible.

Car Repairs—Ah, the age-old debate on whether to buy a newer car that is likely to have fewer problems or an older car that is cheap but may continuously have maintenance issues. Be realistic and know that it's normal for cars to break down and have problems. Plan accordingly.

Car Insurance Premiums—For both of our vehicles, we get hit with a sizable bill every six months. You can opt for monthly bills, but, if you're like me, it's tough to pass up a discount for paying the bill in bigger chunks. If you only pay insurance premiums biannually, be sure to set a calendar reminder so that you are not caught off guard.

Technology—Phones get old and screens crack. TVs break. Laptops crap out. You know these things. Plan for them.

Home Repairs—I already described my horror stories from my first year of home ownership, but I'm hardly an anomaly. Purchasing a home is just the first expense; you are almost guaranteed to have repair costs. And many house-related repairs need to be done ASAP, so you really have no choice but to pay for it. YouTube can save you hundreds or thousands for smaller fixes.

Taxes—If you've ever had a huge, unexpected tax bill (I paid eight thousand dollars one year…), you know how shocking unexpected taxes can be. But if you review your income, your taxes withheld from your paycheck, and your quarterly estimated taxes (if you have side hustle income or are self-employed) throughout the year, rather than just at tax time, you can avoid surprises.[50]

Make sure your emergency fund can handle these "expected" unexpected expenses so that they are nothing more than a speed bump to your finances. It will help you avoid taking out additional debt, either in the form of a credit card or personal loan.

- -

Using your past three months of spending and the 50-30-20 budget as a guideline, go category-by-category and set your budget for next month. Put time on your calendar each week to update and review your spending.

- -

---

50   Quarterly estimated taxes are a confusing topic, especially for those who aren't used to making extra money outside of their 9-5. Here's a resource to help you understand quarterly estimated taxes:StudentLoanSolutionBook.com/QuarterlyTaxes

Strategies and Hacks to Save Money

Some people take saving money to a new level. They'll do anything and everything to spend as little as possible. Whether it's groceries, travel, or furniture—the less they can spend, the better.

If you want to free up cash for saving, investing, and paying down debt, you need to take a good hard look at your spending.

Go step by step through each of your budget spending categories and ask yourself the tough questions. Should you be spending this much? Are there ways you can spend less? **Are you spending your money on things you actually value?**

But you don't have to be obsessive about cutting costs to make an impact on your finances. It's not the most popular suggestion, and I realize not everyone has this option but, for years, my wife and I have packed lunches for work. We deliberately make dinners that will provide leftovers. Now that we are in the habit of doing it, we don't think twice about it. I can honestly count on one hand the number of times I've purchased my lunch at the overpriced work cafeteria the past few years. Though back when I was a summer intern, I did purchase a salad almost every day for lunch. Looking back, I realize I could have saved hundreds if I had just packed a lunch instead! You live and you learn.

Here are some ideas for saving money on various budget categories. These will help you start thinking through what changes you can make in your own life to keep more of your hard-earned money.

Car Loan/Lease

If you have an expensive car with a big monthly payment, can you sell your car and buy a cheaper one? If you lease a car, can you plan ahead for when your lease ends so that you can purchase a more affordable vehicle that you can drive longer?

Auto Repair and Maintenance

Use a coupon when you get an oil change. Shop around for the best rate on repairs, and use a service like Angie's List to find a mechanic with a good reputation. Learn about vehicle maintenance and, if possible, do small repairs/maintenance yourself.

Transportation

Transportation costs are a tough one. We have no control over the cost to fill up our tank, other than how fuel-efficient our vehicle is. Public transportation isn't always convenient (it would take me two hours each way to take the bus to work).

Some options that you could pursue, though, are finally getting the courage to ask to work from home more regularly (if your job allows), find someone to carpool with (this also gives you a good excuse to leave work on time), cut the number of Uber or Lyft rides you take each month, and cut out unnecessary trips.

Cell Phone

Shop around for a more affordable or a similarly priced plan where you get more for your money.

Insurance

- **Auto**
  Look into another insurance company and see if they can give you a better rate for the same coverage. If they will, and you like your current insurer, first ask your current insurance agent about any discounts they offer. Then show them the quote from their competitor (assuming it's better than your current rate) and ask them to match the rate.

- **Health**
  This depends on your personal health situation but, in some cases, choosing to have a higher deductible will make sense and can lower your monthly premiums. If you have a high-deductible health plan, be sure to build a "health emergency fund" through your HSA.

- **Life**
  Look into whether you can get similar coverage for a lower rate. If you can, drop your current coverage and move to the lower-cost coverage. Check and see if your life insurance is "whole" or "term." Whole life insurance has an investment component to it, while term life insurance only pays out if the insured individual passes away while the policy is in place. If you have whole life insurance, ditch it for term life insurance instead.

Cable and Internet

Get rid of cable or satellite ASAP and get a "skinny bundle," which is a slimmed down "cable-like" package. For example, you may get twenty channels for twenty-five dollars a month. The benefit of skinny bundles is that you can cancel and restart your subscription whenever you want, and the costs are much more transparent than traditional cable or satellite. I kept putting off cancelling cable but, once I did, I immediately saw over fifty dollars a month in savings, even after a subscription to Sling TV and Netflix. I don't miss cable.

Ask yourself if you can get by with a digital antenna and no skinny bundle at all. I recommend getting a no-monthly-fee DVR and pairing that with a digital antenna. Shop around for internet, if possible (unfortunately, there is only one company in some areas). If you have unlimited data, see if you can get by with using your cell phone as a Wi-Fi hotspot and cancel both internet and cable!

Focus on Recurring Costs

Peter Anderson, founder of *Bible Money Matters*, suggests focusing first on the highest recurring expenses and working your way down from there.

My recommendation is to put your recurring expenses in order from largest to smallest. Once that's done, work your way backward from the largest to the smallest, and work on finding ways to cut or save on those recurring costs.

For example, for many folks one of their biggest recurring expenses is their mortgage or rent. Look at that one first, and, if you have a mortgage, see if there's a way to refinance into a lower rate, or to cut rate significantly by putting it in a shorter term. Doing that can save you thousands. If you rent, it makes sense to comparison shop and keep your eye out for less expensive, but similar quality, properties.

From there go on down the list to things like homeowners and auto insurance costs, to cell phone bills, entertainment costs, and so on. Start big and get some big wins and go from there.

Clothes

Go through your closet and sell any clothes that you do not wear. Commit to waiting twenty-four hours, forty-eight hours, or some other predetermined amount of time before making any purchases. Ask yourself, "Can I get a similar piece of clothing for less somewhere else? Can I wait until this goes on sale? Do I need this?"

Entertainment

For some people, entertainment is only a tiny portion of their overall spending. For others, though, this can make up a big portion of it. Whether it's movies, concerts, or an expensive hobby like golf or skiing, entertainment costs can add up quick.

I don't believe you need to completely deprive yourself of activities you enjoy simply because you have student loan debt, but I do believe it's worth asking yourself some tough questions. For example, do you *really* enjoy golf enough to justify spending hundreds a month on it? Or can you only go to the movie theater once every four weeks instead of every week? Or can you look for coupons or deals (like five-dollar Tuesday movie nights) that can reduce the amount you spend?

I cut out golf and snowboarding because the amount of money I spent on those activities wasn't worth the entertainment and fun I was getting out of them. There were lower cost and, to be honest, lower time commitment entertainment options that gave me more enjoyment. Questioning your high-cost hobbies could save you a lot of money over time.

Groceries

Groceries are an area where most people can save more money. Grocery stores play a kind of game: they offer discounts, but the only people really benefiting are the ones who put in the time and effort to take advantage of them.

A few things you can do to lower your grocery bill:

- **Meal Plan**—If you just randomly buy groceries and decide on the spot what you are eating at each meal, you can likely save money by creating a meal plan.

- **Make a List**—It's okay to grab a few things that are not on your list, but in general it's a good idea to bring a grocery list to the store and stick to it.

- **Sales and Coupons**—Look at the sales available each week. Is there a store that has lower prices or better deals? For example, are strawberries four dollars a pound at one store and two dollars a pound at another? Or can you get a different fruit that's on sale for less (i.e. buying in-season fruit)?

These tips may seem basic, but if you get in the habit of doing these things, it will become a part of your weekly routine. This is an area in which I have saved thousands of dollars over the past few years. Planning ahead also helps if you are in a relationship because you and your partner don't always have to ask each other every night, "What do you want to eat?" "I don't know, what do you want to eat?"

Also, while we are on the topic of groceries, I can't help but mention buying coffee from a grocery store and brewing it at home. If you stop at Starbucks every morning, even cutting out one or two trips a week can save you a decent amount of money over time.

Gym

In general, you should cancel memberships to save money, but I think that a gym membership is well worth the cost. If you really want to be frugal, you can work out at home or outside, but you need to ask yourself if you are *really* going to do it. If not, it's better to have a gym membership.

Being healthy goes hand-in-hand with being wealthy. When you are healthy, you have more energy and, in general, feel better. You also potentially avoid medical bills that come from being unhealthy (I say this while at the same time recognizing that not all diseases can be prevented simply by exercising and eating well).

Get a gym membership and *actually use it*! If your workplace has a gym or workout room, take advantage of it. Don't be afraid to compare prices, either. You may need daycare and gyms with that option do cost more. If you don't need it, consider a cheaper alternative. If there's a low-cost gym near you (think ten to twenty-five dollars a month), go there.

Travel

There are a ton of different ways to travel on the cheap. I can speak from experience: travelling and spending little money is very fulfilling! I look at travel as a challenge—how can we travel where we want to and spend the smallest amount possible on flights, hotel, and other costs, all while keeping the quality of the trip high? For example, you can use credit card bonuses to get free flights and hotel rooms. You can also plan your trip well in advance and price-compare before booking.

Restaurants/Drinks

I'm a big believer in balancing out working hard, saving money, and socializing. It's great to save money by hosting others and making your own food and drinks, but there is value in going out to restaurants and socializing with friends and family.

With that said, don't sacrifice your budget because of your social life. Decide how much you are willing to spend on restaurants and drinks each month and stick to it. If it means going out less than you are used to, so be it.

Happy hour is usually more affordable so, when that works with your schedule, always suggest it. Picking reasonably priced restaurants helps as well.

One hack I've used is cash-back rewards from credit cards. I've redeemed hundreds of dollars of cash back in the form of Chipotle and Starbucks gift cards. Even though my wife and I go to Chipotle at least once every two weeks, we haven't paid for it out of our own pocket for years. Of course, this only saves you money if you are paying off your credit card in full each month.

Housing

Along with auto and transportation expenses, housing costs are a major expense for most people. Since the housing collapse and recession a decade ago, we have seen the cost of housing increase at a pace that is making home ownership and rent unaffordable for many.

Saving money on housing is all about trade-offs. If you already own a home, it may mean pouring less money into home renovations or going the do-it-yourself route to save money.

DIY is usually not fun (I took on a ridiculous retaining wall project and was completely in over my head), but it can save you thousands. Don't take on anything you aren't comfortable with, though, and prioritize what you can and can't live with. Our bathroom that was in awful shape took precedence over our aging kitchen. Always ask yourself, "How long can I delay this?" Delaying projects equals money in the bank.

If you rent, you need to consider what you care about. Are you willing to commute farther to save money? Or do you care about your location and are willing to trade space for it? Can you stand having a roommate or roommates? What are your "must-haves" in a rental? What are you willing to scrimp on? Rent prices are largely out of your control, but being self-aware about what matters to you can help you make the best choice for you and your finances.

Take five minutes to think about what you care most about when it comes to your monthly expenditures. This can be date nights out with your partner, golf outings on the weekend, the quality of your home/rental, your morning coffee from Starbucks, or anything else.

_____

_____

_____

Now, think about what you don't care about, or at least care *less* about than other things. For me, I don't like spending money on my car (which is why I drive a Kia Spectra!) and going to the movie theater for fifteen dollars a person doesn't feel worth it.

_____

_____

Knowing what you care the most about will help you cut your spending without making yourself miserable.

Now, write down five different ways you can cut your spending, and what you need to do to make it happen. For example:

Expense to Cut	*Action(s)*
Cable	Call my service provider and move to an internet-only plan
	Purchase a digital antenna and DVR.

Expense to Cut	Action(s)

- -

Hustle Your Way to a Higher Income

I'm constantly amazed at the world we live in. Technology has created more opportunities than we can wrap our heads around. We live in a world where you can make money from the comfort of your home—or anywhere there is an internet connection.

One way I made money in college was by working for a blog for a few days a week. It was an awesome side gig. I worked a few hours a week on marketing tasks and could do the work whenever and wherever I wanted.

I've tried many online business ideas that failed. But I learned from each of them, and, when I finally started my personal finance blog *Young Adult Money*, I wanted to make sure I was in it for the long haul. I spent about a year thinking and planning for the site. I knew blogging was a ton of work and didn't want to burn out or quit early on.

Fast forward to today, and not only do I have a profitable blog that has provided me side income, but I've also published a book, *Hustle Away Debt*, that is entirely focused on helping people find the right side hustle for them and optimizing it.

This all connects back to student loans. When my wife and I first received our student loan bills and they totaled $1,000 a month, I was distraught.

I had so many dreams for my life. How could I stomach $1,000 a month for the next ten years? And what about grad school, which could add another $100k or more to our debt?

Those student loan bills motivated me to find a way to make $1,000 a month, or more, to offset the impact. It helped me stick with my blog and pursue other side hustles. I've been hustling for years now, and it's changed my life, not only through extra income, but also because of the new skills I've learned, opportunities I've had, and incredible people I otherwise would not have met.

If an extra $100, $500, $1,000, or more a month would make a big impact on your finances, side hustles may be the jolt your financial life needs.

Side Hustles 101

Side hustles are any way to make extra money above and beyond your nine-to-five. They can be as straightforward as taking on a part-time evening or weekend job or as complex as launching a full-blown business. They can be done entirely online on your own time or may require you to show up at a physical location and clock in and out. They may have guaranteed income (i.e. you work five hours, you get paid seventy-five dollars) or they may never result in any income (that website idea or online business may just never pan out).

The benefit of side hustles is that they can help you reach your financial goals faster. You can only cut your spending so much, and you don't always have control over how much you make at your nine-to-five, but a side hustle is something you can impact. You aren't dependent on the income, and you can choose when to start or stop.

If you have student loans, side hustles can cover your monthly payments, or even help you pay off your loans faster. They can also help you work toward other financial goals that your student loans are holding you back from, like saving for a down payment on a house or paying for your next car in cash.

Before you jump into a side hustle, though, there may be easier ways to improve your finances. And easy is good.

Before You Start That Side Hustle...

Side hustles take time. And what is the one thing most people lack? Time. We all have busy schedules, and if there is one thing we could use more of, it is time.

If you're employed at a nine-to-five, you spend most of your waking hours working, commuting to work, or getting ready for work. How can you possibly find time in your schedule for *more* work?

It's not easy.

And that's why I recommend doing a few things before focusing on a side hustle. Below is what I like to call "the pre-hustle checklist."

1. **Salary Research**
    Are you getting paid a market rate for your job? Do you even know what the market rate is? It's time to do some salary research.

    Researching salaries is easier if you are in a job that is common, like a financial analyst, and is more difficult if your job is very specific or niche. Regardless, you should look at websites like Glassdoor or PayScale where salary data is crowdsourced. If the company you work for is big enough, you can even see where you stand among others in a similar role at your company.

2. **Look at Job Openings at the Next Level**
    Are you qualified for a job at the next level? What sort of skills or experience are companies looking for at the next

level? These are questions that you should either know the
answer to or should look into.

I recommend that people look at job openings regularly,
at least once a quarter. This will keep you up to speed
on what employers are looking for and give you time to
develop the skills and experience necessary to get to the
next level. When you look at job openings, you may be
surprised to see you already have the skills and experience
employers are looking for.

3. **Apply for New Jobs and/or Ask for a Raise**
   Based on your salary and job research, you may realize
   that now is the time to act by either having a conversation
   about compensation at your current employer or applying
   to open jobs.

   If you need motivation, realize that it can be a lot easier to
   make an extra five or ten thousand dollars at your nine-to-
   five than through a side hustle. Because, let's be honest:
   often the people who make more money aren't working
   that much longer than entry-level employees. And typically
   moving up one level does not translate to significantly
   more hours worked per week, if any at all. I personally
   know people who have gone through the process of
   reviewing salary data and requesting a raise, and because
   of these actions received sizable pay increases that had a
   big impact on their finances. It's worth having the tough
   conversations.

   Alissa Carpenter, millennial workforce expert and
   leadership trainer, believes a specific focus on quantifiable
   numbers can give you a better chance of success. She
   says, "Sometimes, numbers speak louder than words
   and this case is no exception. The key is to show how

your contributions have enhanced the organization and why investing in you will lead to continual growth for your organization."

4. **Did your manager say no?** Despite the disappointment that comes with not receiving a pay increase, it's not the end of the road. Carpenter has some additional action items you can take: "Sit down with your supervisor and have a conversation about the criteria they are looking for in order to earn a raise. Are there specific sales numbers you need to reach or a leadership responsibility they would like to observe? From there, ask for their suggestions for professional development opportunities to help you gain knowledge, skills, and experiences. This might be taking a course, getting a certification, or attending a leadership program. Then ask them if they would be willing to review your request in six months. At that point, you will have worked toward the goals outlined with your supervisor and they will have a broader picture of what you can accomplish."

The follow-up conversation may not be the most comfortable conversation, either, but it forces your employer to define specific goals and targets. This helps in the next conversation, as you can show you accomplished those actions.

5. **Review Your Spending**
If you passed over the money-saving tips from the last section, go back through it and give it some serious thought. While you inevitably will get to a point where you can't cut back any further without being miserable, it can be much easier to cut out two hundred dollars than to make an additional two hundred dollars in side hustles. This goes back to time. Cutting two hundred dollars a

month may cost you nothing in terms of additional time commitments, but side hustles will always take from your free time.

6. **Interest Rate on Your Debt**
   You may roll your eyes at me yet again bringing up interest rates, but it does matter. If you can save one hundred dollars a month on interest, that's one hundred dollars of cash flow that you just freed up that can be put toward your debt, savings, or other financial goals. If you have credit card or other high-interest debt, see if you can refinance at a lower interest rate.

Go through the pre-hustle checklist. Even if you do everything on the pre-hustle checklist, you can still side hustle; your side hustle dollars will just go that much further, though, since you already improved your cash flow prior to pursuing one.

Side Hustle Ideas

There's no shortage of opportunities to make extra money outside of your nine-to-five. I'm no longer surprised when I hear of someone doing something in their spare time to supplement their income. It's becoming more common.

For example, when I was shooting a few segments for an NBC affiliate, the reporter and I started talking to a tech person on set. He ended up revealing that, in his spare time, he likes to work on his model railroad. But that wasn't the surprising part of the story. The surprising part was that he received six hundred dollars per article that he wrote for a model railroad website. Here I was talking about side hustles and someone on set had a lucrative one himself!

I've included a big list of side hustles to help you start brainstorming. Ultimately, there is no limit to what you can do. You need to pick one that plays to your strengths, is enjoyable enough to do in your spare time, and provides the income you are looking for.

Quick-Money Side Hustles

- Deliver food through an app
- Drive for Uber or Lyft
- Work at a retail store
- Wait tables at a restaurant
- Bartend
- Sell plasma

Local Side Hustles

- Babysit
- House sit
- Pet sit
- Walk dogs
- Landscape
- Care for the elderly
- Tutor
- Mystery shop
- Host an Airbnb

- Flip things on eBay or Craigslist
- Referee
- Coach
- DJ
- Bake or cook
- Photograph for weddings, babies, or other special occasions
- Shoot and edit video
- Be a fitness instructor
- Be a personal trainer
- Teach a class
- Shop for others (i.e. clothes, food, etc.)
- Create custom furniture

Online/Remote Side Hustles

- Freelance write
- Edit
- Do graphic design
- Blog
- Podcast
- Record voiceovers
- Create YouTube videos
- Complete taxes
- Work as a spreadsheet consultant
- Work as a database consultant
- Manage social media

- Provide customer service over phone or chat
- Create an online course
- Program websites or apps
- Design websites
- Create and sell Excel spreadsheet templates
- Create and sell PowerPoint templates
- Travel hack
- Do random tasks as a virtual assistant
- Enter giveaways and sell your winnings
- Translate
- Transcribe
- Review and edit resumes
- Coach clients (career, life, etc.)
- Perform user testing
- Take surveys/give your opinion
- Conduct affiliate marketing
- Find, organize, and use coupons
- Flip websites
- Sell your photos
- Sell your music
- Moderate forums

Small Business Side Hustles

- Create a physical or virtual product to sell
- Start an Etsy store

- Create an app
- Create a website and sell advertising, a product, or a service

There are likely thousands of side hustles out there, including many that are obscure or niche. When brainstorming side hustles that may be a good fit for you, don't limit yourself to this list.

Picking the Right Side Hustle for You

If you decide to pursue a side hustle to increase your income, you may find yourself experiencing decision paralysis. There are so many options available that it may be difficult to choose one. Reading through the big list of side hustles may have helped bring ideas to the forefront of your mind but may not have helped you choose a specific one to focus on.

Here's a few questions that you should ask yourself:

What commitments do you already have? What can and can't be dropped?

_____

_____

_____

_____

_____

_____

For example, if you have children, it makes side hustles that require you to be physically present more difficult, unless a partner can watch them. You also don't want to miss out on time with them. A remote or virtual side hustle, perhaps one that you can start and stop when you want, may be ideal. Or, if you are a stay-at-home parent, you could watch one or two extra kids. Doing this even part-time or sporadically could provide a decent income stream.

Another way to think of this is: What is your capacity? If you realistically can only dedicate four or five hours a week to a side hustle, or can only sporadically dabble in it, you need to factor that in when deciding which one to pursue.

How quickly do you need to make extra income?

_____

_____

_____

If you are in a tough spot where you need immediate cash, you may need to pursue a "quick cash" side hustle that requires you to clock in and clock out. Having a second job at a department store or elsewhere isn't the sexiest thing, but you know exactly how much you are going to make. Plus, you can start making money immediately.

On the flip side, if you don't need the extra money right away, you could pursue a "long tail" side hustle that may not make any money immediately but can be lucrative over time, like freelance writing, blogging, photography/videography, etc.

What skills do you have that you could translate into a service that you charge clients for?

_____

_____

_____

_____

_____

This is why freelance writing comes to mind for so many people when they are initially brainstorming side hustles. College grads, especially those with liberal arts degrees, typically spend many hours on papers and other writing-related assignments.

I would encourage you to think outside the box, if possible. For example, do you have knowledge of a specific topic that you can coach or tutor others on? Even something simple like teaching guitar could turn out to be an easy fifty dollars-an-hour side hustle. A couple of side hustles unique to me and my skill set include creating spreadsheets for a small business and creating spreadsheets for my website. Think about what specific skills you have that can be monetized.

What is your long-term goal with this side hustle?

_____

_____

_____

_____

_____

I know a couple who spent nearly two years serving on the weekends to help pay for their wedding in cash. They did this on top of their nine-to-five jobs. It was a grind, but they had a specific goal and end date. Having a specific goal and timeline can make an otherwise "grind" of a side hustle tolerable.

On the flip side, if your ultimate goal is to create a sizable income stream or business that could potentially replace your nine-to-five, it makes sense to think through what side hustles could actually result in that outcome.

Kevin Ha, founder of *The Financial Panther* personal finance blog, started a side hustle delivering through the company Postmates specifically because he was able to do the deliveries without a car; everything could be done with a bike. "The great thing is that biking was something I was already doing for fun and exercise anyway, which meant that I was essentially getting paid to bike. The flexibility worked out perfectly for me as well since I could just turn on the app and do deliveries whenever I had free time." Notice how he found a side hustle that worked with his current lifestyle.

Here is some advice Ha offers for those looking to start a side hustle:

> One strategy to picking side hustles is to pick ones that are low-cost to get started and that you can easily incorporate into your day.

> A low-cost side hustle is important because it gives you the flexibility to switch things up if you find out that a particular side hustle isn't for you. If you invest a lot of time and money into a side hustle, you can still switch things up if you find out it's not for you, but you'll also be out the money that you invested into it.

> Finding side hustles that you can incorporate into your day-to-day routine is important as well. We all have limited hours in the day, so if you can find a side hustle that incorporates things you're already doing, you'll be able to side hustle without losing tons of time.

Jason Butler, founder of the personal finance blog *The Butler Journal*, has a successful eBay side hustle. An eBay side hustle may not be as easy to start as a delivery gig, and certainly has a learning curve, but virtually anyone can go to thrift stores and garage sales and find things to sell. The key is finding the right things. Butler says his most popular items are Jordan shoes, sports jerseys, and the board game Cash Flow.

To get started, Butler suggests starting with what you know. "The fastest way to get started is to figure out what you want to sell and list it. Everyone has something that they know. For me, it was sports, so I started with jerseys and Jordans. Sign up for eBay, take good pictures and list your items ASAP." Butler lost some money on sales as he was figuring out how things work, so if you do choose eBay, recognize there is a learning curve. My wife has also sold many things on eBay, and she also faced the learning curve, including losing money on a couple of sales.

What side hustle will you pursue?

_____

How long will you work this side hustle—a set timeline or indefinitely?

_____

When will you work your side hustle? I recommend carving out specific time in your calendar.

_____

_____

_____

The Unexpected Upside of Side Hustles

It's not natural for us to think of the total cost of our decisions. It's why many of us haven't questioned the full cost of plastic bags or plastic straws, at least until recently. Or why many of us don't factor in the added costs that come with owning a home instead of renting.

In the same way, we don't always think about the potential upside of things. Side hustles are no different. One of my favorite things to talk about with side hustles isn't how to get started or the variety of different ways to make money. It's how people simply started something, and it turned into something they couldn't have possibly imagined.

Being a blogger, it should be no surprise that I know many people who have left their nine-to-five jobs to be full-time freelancers and business owners, often making the same or more (sometimes significantly more) than they were at their nine-to-five. And it's not just writers and bloggers, but other creatives who have taken the plunge to do full-time videography, music production, or a variety of other services.

Besides leaving a nine-to-five job, there is additional upside to pursuing a side hustle, including:

- **Learning and Developing Skills**
  The more you practice something, the better you get. For me, my spreadsheet-focused side hustle helped at my nine-to-five because I was spending time outside of work practicing and improving skills I used every day at work. Another example is tutoring someone who is trying to learn a foreign language. It's an opportunity to get paid to practice your language skills—an opportunity you may

otherwise lack. Getting paid to learn and develop skills is a
pretty good gig.

Depending on the experience you gain, your side hustle
could result in a career pivot that you were interested
in, but otherwise would have never been considered for.
It can result in a raise because you feel more confident
having the tough conversations with your manager about
compensation when you know you have side hustle income
to fall back on. Salary and promotion conversations are
much more difficult when you are scared of riling up the
status quo, which can be the case when your nine-to-five is
your sole source of income.

- **Receiving A Lump Sum Payout**
  You may be able to exit your side hustle with a lump
  sum of cash in hand if the business or website you create
  has even moderate success. This upside is limited to the
  more business-type side hustles where you are building
  something.

- **Being Exposed to New Opportunities**
  There was a time when I seriously considered selling my
  personal finance blog *Young Adult Money*. Blogging is a
  grind, and it's something that you continually have to work
  on and push forward. I decided against it and, just a few
  months later, signed my first book deal. Simply keeping my
  blog updated and sticking with it has resulted in potentially
  life-changing opportunities. I know other people who have
  similar stories with their side hustles.

- **Developing New Relationships**
  You never know who you will meet through a side hustle,
  or what impact they will have on your life. Even if it's "just"
  working an extra job at a retail store or in food services,

you never know what chance meeting you may have. You could meet lifelong friends or a future business partner or client (and, not to get your hopes up, even a partner).

Creating an extra income stream in your free time isn't the easiest thing. It can be physically and mentally draining. But there is upside above and beyond simply making extra money, and, if you decide to pursue an extra income stream, I'd encourage you to use that as motivation to stick with it.

Master Your Credit

Just like budgeting, your credit is something that comes up again and again in personal finance. At its core, your credit history tells lenders how reliable or risky you are as a borrower. Not surprisingly, if you have a long history of on-time payments, you are more likely to have a high credit score than if you have a history of missing required payments.

Your credit impacts the interest rate you get on loans and, in some cases, even the ability to get a loan or a credit card. It's a reason why private student loans for undergrad students typically have a cosigner; the student applying rarely has enough credit history to justify the lender making the loan.

In step one, I mentioned that your credit report would be the place to look if you don't know who owns your private student loans. But pulling your credit report is something you should do annually, regardless of whether you have private student loans. You are entitled to a free credit report from each of the reporting agencies (Equifax, TransUnion, and Experian) once a year. You can get your free credit report at annualcreditreport.com.

Your credit report influences your credit score, or FICO score. They are not the same thing. Your credit report lists your outstanding debt and things like late payments, defaults, bankruptcies, etc. Your credit score is a number that ranges from 300 to 850. As a general guideline, here's what each range means:

<500: Very Bad

500-549: Bad

550-599: Poor

600-649: Fair

650-699: Good

700-749: Very Good

750 and up: Excellent

There are a lot of myths around what helps or hurts your credit score. I've heard many people ask questions based on these myths or just plain misinformation about credit scores.

The easiest way to understand what will help or hurt your credit score is by looking at what impacts your credit score.

35 percent Payment History

30 percent Amount Owed

15 percent Length of Credit History

10 percent New Credit Applications

10 percent Types of Credit

- **Payment History**

  Because payment history has such a huge impact on your credit score, you should always make your minimum debt payments on time. This is one reason why I think an emergency fund is important. An emergency fund ensures that you will have extra money set aside in case you hit a rough patch. You will at least be able to continue making your payments on time. It's also worth noting that the further behind you are on payments, the more detrimental the impact to your credit.

- **Amount Owed**

  The amount of debt you have relative to your available credit, also referred to as credit utilization, impacts your credit score. For example, if you have $5,000 of available credit but you have a balance of $4,500, your utilization is relatively high. Utilizing 30 percent or less of your available credit is recommended.

- **Length of Credit History**

  Length of credit history is where people get tripped up. Some people believe that having just one or two credit cards helps their credit score, and therefore they should close their credit cards before opening a new one. If you have a credit card for ten years with no annual fee, do not close it! Your credit score will factor in how old your oldest credit is as well as the average age of your credit.

- **New Credit Applications**

  When you apply for a new line of credit, the lender will usually do a "hard inquiry" into your credit. This can cause a temporary negative impact to your credit score. Lenders will view you, at least in theory, as a bigger risk because you recently opened new lines of credit. This is a relatively small impact, at 10 percent, but it's why you may

have heard the advice to not open new credit when you
are thinking about buying a home and, in turn, taking out
a mortgage.

- **Types of Credit**
  Lenders like to see a variety of credit. For example,
  installment plans like student loans and auto loans in
  combination with credit cards. This is a small component
  of your credit score, at 10 percent, so do not use it as
  justification for increasing your variety of debt.

Improving Your Credit Score

There are a number of ways to improve your credit score and
keep it moving in the right direction. They include:

- **Checking Your Credit Report for Errors**
  If your credit score dropped unexpectedly, there's a chance
  that there is an error on your credit report. If you find
  one, you should report it immediately. Rachel Slifka, a
  freelance writer and contributor to *Young Adult Money*,
  made a great analogy stressing the urgency: "If someone
  broke into your house, you would be sure to report it. If
  something is inaccurate on your credit report, you should
  also report it."

  All three credit bureaus (Experian, TransUnion, and
  Equifax) accept online credit disputes. Go to the bureau's
  website and fill out and submit an online dispute form.
  Be sure to include any documentation that supports your
  dispute. The more specific you can be about what you are
  disputing and what action should be taken, the easier it
  will be for the bureau to correct it.

- **Make Payments on Time**

  On-time payments are vital for a good credit score. Getting your debt current is important, so even if you are behind on payments, don't stop making payments altogether. Show your lender that you are trying and use that as leverage to negotiate an arrangement that gets your debt current.

  Automating your payment is one way to avoid forgetting to make a payment. However, if you do this, you will want to make sure that your checking account is at a level where there is no risk of an overdraft.

- **Lower Your Credit Utilization**

  If you are carrying a balance on your credit card, not only are you paying high interest, but it also may be hurting your credit score if your credit utilization is 30 percent or greater. Your long-term goal should be to pay off your credit card debt in full, but, short-term, you should look to get the balance below 30 percent. If you pay off the balance on your credit card each month (which is ideal), be cognizant of how much of a balance you have at any given time, and make sure it's always less than 30 percent.

- **Use a Credit Booster Loan**

  There's a decent percentage of college grads who have never had a credit card. While this can be a good thing because it means they don't have credit card debt, it also can cause a low or, in some cases, nonexistent credit score (not enough info to assign a score).

  This has caused a new product to come to market called a credit-builder loan. There are a variety of banks and companies offering these today. One company I looked into has a plan where you get a loan for around a thousand dollars and make monthly loan payments for twelve months, with the company making monthly reports to all three credit bureaus.[51]

Implications for Student Loan Borrowers

Student loans are not inherently bad for your credit score, which many are happy to hear. But that's only the case if you make on-time payments. If a lender sees that you have been making years of on-time payments, it's a good indicator that you are a reliable borrower. This is the exact situation my wife and I found when we were looking into getting a mortgage. We had a lot of student loan debt, but years of on-time payments made for solid credit scores.

One specific thing related to student loans that can impact your credit score: if you are on an IDR plan, your payment may not cover all your interest. There are interest benefits on some of the IDR plans, but, even so, your principal is not going down. Lenders like to see your principal go down over time, not increase.

The benefits of IDR are numerous, including likelihood of staying current on your payments, but it's worth noting that this could be a negative aspect of taking on IDR. If this scenario fits you, my recommendation is to be more diligent in pursuing strategies for improving your credit score.

---

51   You can read more about this here: StudentLoanSolutionBook.com/CreditBuilder

Key Takeaways

- Keeping a budget is an important way to gain control over your money and your financial life.

- Choose a budget tool and process that work for you.

- Review your budget and spending at least once a month. In the beginning, review them weekly to see how your spending is tracking against your budget for the month.

- Look for opportunities to save money and cut expenses. Focus on cutting things you don't value as much. Make sure your discretionary spending is focused on things you value.

- A side hustle can be a great way to increase your income. An extra income stream has unexpected upside above and beyond simply providing you with extra income.

- Before you start a side hustle, focus on things that may be easier and quicker wins for your finances, like increasing your income at your nine-to-five and cutting expenses.

- Understanding and keeping tabs on your credit report and credit score are worthwhile because of how they impact future financial decisions like taking out a mortgage or refinancing student loans. Take the necessary actions to improve your credit and you should see your score rise over time.

Bonus Section: Your Student Loans and Your Life

There is so much that can be said about how student loans impact specific life situations. Because student loans touch so many areas of a borrower's life, there is a never-ending list of topics that could be unpacked. What I want to do in this bonus section is to hit on a few of the more common, and in my opinion, important, areas of our lives that student loans impact.

We'll first dive into the topic of mental health, which I think is extremely important, considering the psychological toll that student loans can take. Next, we'll discuss relationships and the potential negative impact that student loans can have on them, including what to do if they impact your relationship. We'll continue to discuss relationships by addressing weddings, especially how to go about planning your finances for this potentially budget-busting cost. Finally, we will talk about something that is common not just with people who have student loans, but many workers: what to do if you hate your job or career. This is particularly difficult for people with student loans, because you may feel guilt at just the thought of leaving a job or career that you went into debt for.

Let's get to it!

Student Loans and Your Mental Health

In general, student loans have a negative impact on mental health. A study published in the journal *Social Science & Medicine* in 2015 found a correlation between student loans and poorer psychological functioning.[52] If you have student loans, especially a large amount, this likely doesn't come as a surprise. It's well known that debt correlates with stress and anxiety.

Dr. Katrina Walsemann, one of the study authors, speculates that it's the permanent nature of student loans that makes them so stress-inducing.[53] They are a unique sort of debt in the sense that you can't just walk away from them; they stay with you until they are paid off. They are extremely difficult to discharge through bankruptcy, unlike credit card and other forms of debt. When you default on student loans, typically, you exit default with a bigger bill. With other forms of debt, when you fall behind, you can typically negotiate or have a professional negotiate a lower, more reasonable amount to repay.

Each year, around a million borrowers default on federal student loans for the first time.[54] If you're in default or have gone through default, you know how stressful a situation it can be. Even borrowers who are current on their loans are at risk of stress, anxiety, and shame around their debt. I strongly believe student loan debt is something people suffer with silently. It's something that isn't commonly discussed, and, when it is discussed, the conversation is rarely met with empathy from those who either have never had debt or have paid theirs off already.

I've stressed the idea of control throughout this book. Taking control of your student debt and, more broadly, of your finances

52   Walsemann, Katrina; Gee, Gilbert; Gentile, Danielle. "Sick of our loans: Student borrowing and the mental health of young adults in the United States," *Social Science & Medicine*, https://www.sciencedirect.com/science/article/pii/S0277953614007503. Volume 124, January 2015.

53   University of South Carolina. "How are student loans affecting the well-being of young adults?" *ScienceDaily*, https://www.sciencedaily.com/releases/2015/01/150122114430.htm. 22 January 2015.

54   Based on data from the National Student Loan Data System https://catalog.data.gov/dataset/national-student-loan-data-system

is an important step for every borrower. Know your options. Understand your situation. Pick a strategy. Take action.

Being in control of your situation is helpful, but let's not be naïve; even if you've done all the work and are on a repayment plan, anxiety, stress, and depression can still occur. Simply having a large amount of debt hanging over your head can weigh on you regardless of progress you've made toward repaying it.

Melanie Lockert, author of *Dear Debt: A Story about Breaking Up with Debt*, says, "It's crucial we acknowledge the correlation between debt and depression and break down barriers around these two topics. When you're so depressed and anxious, you get paralyzed. Having a conversation, getting help, and setting up a plan can help you take the steps required to get out of debt."

Lockert had a particularly eye-opening experience that underscored just how serious this issue is: "A few years ago I found out many people were coming to my blog because they searched 'I want to kill myself because of debt.' I was gutted and heartbroken over this. So, I decided to write about it. After writing about my own experience, I got emails from others in student loan debt who were suffering, some on the brink of suicide. I've realized that debt is very personal and that no two people feel the same about their debt. I've also realized that many student loan borrowers feel depressed because of debt. They feel like their life is on hold and they're not sure what to do."

This is obviously difficult to read, but it is the reality of the situation. There are individuals suffering greatly from debt. If you are experiencing anxiety, stress, or depression stemming from your student loan debt, or any other reason, please speak with a professional. Being married to a therapist, I can tell you they spend countless hours, both in the classroom and in practice, so that they have the appropriate skill set and expertise to help you. Lockert also recommends speaking to a counselor if student loans are affecting your daily life and mental health: "I received affordable counseling at the local graduate school for five dollars per session (which I negotiated down from fifteen dollars per session)."

Besides finding a counselor in your area, you can also contact these organizations and resources:

- Crisis Text Line: Text 741741

- National Suicide Prevention Lifeline: 1-800-273-8255

- Open Path Collective: https://openpathcollective.org/

- Project Semicolon: https://projectsemicolon.com/

- National Foundation for Credit Counseling: https://www.nfcc.org/

Saying our society isn't the best at taking care of our mental health is an understatement. We are conditioned to push ourselves to the brink and put anything related to mental health under the rug. We can't afford to continue to treat it as a low priority. If you are experiencing symptoms of depression, it's important to talk to a professional. Instead of putting it at the bottom of your to-do list, move it to the top. Don't give all your attention to other aspects of your health, such as your physical and financial health. It all connects. You deserve good mental health!

Student Loans and Your Relationships

Money is a taboo topic. It's difficult to force yourself to "get real" with your finances. It's easy to put off looking into what debt you have, what it will take to pay it off, and what changes are needed to get on track. But when you bring someone else into the equation and you have no idea how they will respond to your student loan debt, it's even more difficult. You have a lot riding on them reacting positively. You are being vulnerable and putting yourself out there, knowing there's a risk they won't be as understanding as you hope.

Student loans have a unique impact on relationships, but money and finances in general have always been a driver of stress. 43 percent of couples fight about money at least "somewhat often," according to a Student Loan Hero survey of over a thousand student loan borrowers[55], and, in a survey by SunTrust Bank, 35 percent of respondents who were experiencing relationship stress said that money was the primary cause.[56] Even more alarming is the number of divorces that cite student loans specifically as the reason: 13 percent.[57]

Being vulnerable is important in a relationship, and so is knowing your value. It's a reason why I'm so passionate about personal finance. Having control over your money will give you confidence in other areas of your life, from careers to relationships.

You deserve someone who values you regardless of your financial situation.

---

55   Insler, Shannon. "Debt in the Bedroom: Survey Shows 32 percent of Student Loan Borrowers Report Decreased Libido," *Student Loan Hero*, https://studentloanhero. com/featured/debt-bedroom-survey-shows-student-loan-borrowers-report-decreased-libido/. March 2018.

56   "First Comes Love, Then Comes…Money Squabbles?" *SunTrust*, https://www. suntrust.com/resource-center/personal-finances/article/first-comes-love-then-comes-money-squabbles.

57   Luthi, Ben. "Survey: Student Loan Borrowers Wait Longer and Pay More to Get Divorced," *Student Loan Hero*, https://studentloanhero.com/featured/survey-student-loan-borrowers-and-divorce/. August 2018.

I have heard single people who I otherwise respect and admire say they would not date someone who has significant student loan debt. While student loan debt is an important thing to wrap your head around and have a solid plan for, if there is someone who is shallow enough to assign value to you based on your level of debt, student or otherwise, it's a huge red flag. **You deserve better.**

It's Critical to Be on the Same Page with Your Partner When It Comes to Debt

When my wife and I went through pre-marriage counseling, the leader of the session had a daughter who was divorced. Based on the stories he told, it sounded like the approach his daughter and her partner took with money was that specific bills and financial responsibilities were assigned to one or the other. When she lost her job, her husband said that the car bill was her problem and she needed to figure out how she would pay it.

I don't know about you, but that doesn't sound like much of a partnership. Is it really any surprise they eventually divorced?

Debt is a hot topic today, and there are many couples who bring vastly different debt to their marriage. Some finance experts, including some who I greatly respect, will tell you to have a prenuptial agreement so that the partner who is bringing less debt to the marriage will not be responsible for partner debt—or will be credited for payments made toward it—if the marriage fails.

If both partners are on the same page, I think this might be okay. But I'm conflicted. Shouldn't a marriage have a team approach to problems? By taking this approach, won't one partner always feel like the potential for divorce could be used as leverage against them, since they will be in a worse-off financial situation?

Elle Martinez, founder of *Couple Money* and author of *Jumpstart Your Marriage and Your Money*, says, "Whether you go with a prenup or not, I think the bigger question is 'why?' Why do they think it is necessary? It very well could be, but the conversation is crucial to figuring if it is in the best interest of their relationship. If it is a trust issue (a partner is concerned he or she could be being used), I would recommend they get marital counseling *before* they walk down the aisle. Sometimes that's hard to admit out loud, but it's something that needs to be addressed."

Martinez does not think that protecting the partner with less personal debt is enough of a reason to justify getting a prenup. "For example, what if one partner has little debt because their parents took care of college expenses while the other worked through their degree? What if one spouse is a physician and has a mountain of debt, but will soon be making significant money? What if one spouse was a single parent and accumulated debt trying to stay afloat—but they are now working toward paying it off?"

Regardless of how you and your partner decide to deal with finances, you must be on the same page. If you aren't 100 percent comfortable with the approach, you need to discuss your concerns with your partner. For example, if you are not in favor of a prenup but your partner thinks it's absolutely necessary, your concern is just as valid as theirs.

Ultimately, if your finances are a deal breaker for your partner, it may be time to find a new partner. Why? Because I know you are serious about your money. You are reading a book on how to tackle your student loans, after all!

You Need to Be Open about Your Financial Situation

24 percent of student loan borrowers have kept their student loans a secret from their partner.[58] Nearly one out of four.

If you are keeping your student loans secret from a partner you are serious about, you need to have a conversation with them ASAP. This is for both their sake and yours. A lot will be revealed about a person by how they react to you putting your financials on the table. If you have a lot of debt they did not know about, they may react negatively and be stressed out at first, but if they don't show respect and have a "team" mentality soon after the initial reaction, it's a red flag.

This is a two-way street. Your partner needs to also be willing to put themselves out there and be truthful and open about their financials. This is someone you may be moving toward committing to spending the rest of your life with or have already committed to. You cannot be on the same page financially if you don't both put yourselves out there.

There's a chance that your partner has treated you poorly because of your finances. To reiterate what I said earlier: **this is not okay!**

If you find yourself being treated poorly due to your financial situation, Martinez thinks a third party is necessary: "At the very least you need to get a professional third party involved, such as a certified financial planner or a financial therapist with a specialty working with couples. Provided this is not a

---

58   Insler, Shannon. "Debt in the Bedroom: Survey Shows 32 percent of Student Loan Borrowers Report Decreased Libido," *Student Loan Hero*, https://studentloanhero.com/featured/debt-bedroom-survey-shows-student-loan-borrowers-report-decreased-libido/. March 2018.

safety and/or a physical abuse issue (in which case you should seek help as necessary), the therapist or planner may be able to objectively diagnose the root of this hostility. If both individuals are on board, the financial planner or therapist can also provide specific resources tailored for the couple, so they can break this cycle and start having healthier communication and build up their finances."

How the Hell Do I Pay for This Wedding?

We can't talk about student loans and relationships without talking about a major expense that usually comes with them: weddings. I'll start by stating the obvious: just like a college education, we can't all go to the Bank of Mom and Dad and cash out a free wedding. Some of us have to pay for all or most of it ourselves.

There are two common scenarios when it comes to student loans and weddings. One is the couple who got engaged before their senior year, blissfully unaware of the student loan debt that would drop a giant deuce on their picture-perfect life six months after graduation. The second is the couple who got engaged and are aware of the burden of their student loans. Going into debt to pay for a wedding may feel irresponsible to this couple; the drain their loans put on their finances might make them wonder how the heck they can come up with thousands of dollars for a wedding.

The good news is that you are reading this book. You want to improve your finances. You want to find solutions. Here are a few suggestions:

Create a Wedding Budget

Find out what you realistically need for your wedding. I created a wedding budget spreadsheet for a friend and put it online for others to use as well. You can get it at StudentLoanSolutionBook. com/WeddingBudget.

Fill in all the projected costs. Get quotes if you need to. The total may be alarming, especially if you are getting no help from family, but it's pointless to go through this exercise unless you are being honest with yourself.

Decide What Matters to You

The next step will be figuring out where you are willing to cut costs and what matters to you as a couple. Chonce Maddox, founder of the personal finance blog *My Debt Epiphany* and creator of a resource guide on saving money on your wedding, thinks it's important to block out everyone's opinion but your own.

> If you're a couple looking to save money on your wedding, you should take a step back and identify your joint values and ideas for the wedding. Notice I said "YOUR." When people get engaged, it's natural for friends and family to be excited, but sometimes they push their own values and ideas on you for your special day. The day is about the two of you and not about making anyone else happy.

> Make a list of what's super important to you and a list of what isn't. You may need to compromise but rank your list in order of importance. Doing this will allow you to focus on guiltlessly spending money on that top value and spending less on the rest.

Have People Pay for Parts of Your Honeymoon as a Wedding Gift

Allow people to give traditional gifts, but if you don't want stuff for your house or apartment and feel bad asking for money instead of gifts, create a honeymoon itinerary that people can sponsor. I know a couple who did this for their honeymoon to Europe, and it worked out great. They listed things like train rides, hotel stays, etc., that people could contribute toward as their gift. For bigger items, like plane tickets, have options to sponsor portions of it (i.e. twenty-five dollars, fifty dollars, etc.).

Side Hustle

I mentioned earlier the couple who waited tables on the weekends to pay for their wedding in cash. While working every day of the week between your nine-to-five and side hustle may not sound attractive, it helps if you have a specific target dollar amount (i.e. your wedding budget) that you are shooting for. You know there is an end date. You won't be working the extra hours forever, and sometimes knowing that is enough to grind out the work in the short term.

Maddox also thinks getting a side hustle to help cover wedding expenses is a smart idea. "You'll want to choose something that will pay you well for your time, so taking surveys online probably won't cut it. I've been able to earn thousands per month by freelance writing on the side when I was planning my wedding and that's the type of money you'll need to make depending on your budget." Some additional ideas she gives are virtual assistant work, web design, coding, and driving for Uber or Lyft.

There's no magical way to get rid of all the costs that go with a wedding, and if your family doesn't have money to help, it's unlikely that will change. What you can do is focus on prioritizing

what you spend money on and cutting costs on things you don't
care about. Do-it-yourself is always a good option, though I
still gripe about the twenty steps it took to put together each of
our DIY invitations...but in all seriousness, saving money is a
good feeling!

Student Loans and Your Career–I Hate What I'm Doing!

Have you ever thought, "I wish I was doing something different
with my life, but I have all these student loans..."

You aren't alone.

Social media doesn't help. You may see others living lives you
wish you were living, whether it's having a job that allows them
to travel, running a business full-time, or just working in a field
they actually like. Many books could be written on the societal
and psychological impacts of social media, but I think most
would agree that it's made more and more people ask, "What am
I doing with my life?"

We also live in a time when technology has made it easier than
ever to make extra money on top of a full-time job, including
testing out business and self-employment ideas. While it's
ultimately a positive thing, the ability to test out different ways
of making income can cause people to second-guess their career
choice and question the lack of control they may feel in their
current job.

A source of frustration for some is how slow their employer is
to pick up on trends. We still have millions of people going into

offices just to sit on their laptop in their cubicle, doing work that can be done anywhere there is an internet connection. Additionally, some jobs do not need to be done during a set time period, yet standard work hours persist at most companies.

Regardless of the reason, you may have thought about switching careers, taking a lower-paying job, or even giving entrepreneurship a try. Sitting in an office grinding away the days may be difficult for you, knowing there is something else you think you should be doing with your life.

So why don't you just *do it*?

If you have student loans, and in some situations even if you don't, there are a few things that may be holding you back:

- You don't want to take a job that pays less than your current one.

- You feel guilty about leaving a job and career that you went into debt for.

- You fear the unknown.

Underlying all of these is *money*. How much we make, how much we have, and what we've used it for in the past (like a degree you may no longer want). This all goes back to our money mindset, too, because how we view money will impact how we move forward in life.

It's important for you to give yourself permission to not stay in a line of work you don't enjoy. We spend countless hours each year working, and those hours add up to a huge number over the course of a career. Just because you got a degree and started working in one field does not mean you have to stay in that job or field forever. This doesn't mean you should quit your job tomorrow. What it does mean is perhaps starting to move in a new direction. Consider taking some practical steps that will help you pivot into a new career or line of work that you enjoy and that is fulfilling.

I'm going to greatly oversimplify the variables that go into pursuing a new line of work, but here are a few things that I think are worth considering as you look toward a new line of work.

Become Money Savvy

There's no getting around it: when you don't feel financially secure, you will hesitate to take risks and will err on the side of playing it safe. Someone who has one hundred thousand dollars of student loans with a thirty-thousand-dollar emergency fund is going to make a decision differently than someone who has the same amount of student loans but no emergency fund.

Reading this book was a big step forward toward becoming savvy about money. But it can't stop here. Keeping your budget for the next month, two months, and two years is important. So is consistently building that emergency fund, looking for ways to increase your income and to save money. You need to keep doing these things month after month. Slowly (and in some cases, quickly) you will move toward better financial security and confidence around how you manage your money and your financial situation.

Being financially savvy will help you pay off your debt faster and/ or manage your cash flow better. For example, if your monthly student loans were unaffordable but you were unaware of IDR plans, you likely would be headed toward default. Understanding IDR and loan forgiveness may change the way you approach your career and even the way you think about your job. Someone in a PSLF qualified nonprofit may be much more content with their job knowing they are working toward loan forgiveness and setting themselves up for success long-term. In contrast, someone who doesn't know about PSLF may just see themselves as an underpaid worker who won't ever be able to dig themselves out of debt.

Reflect Often on Where You Want to Be

So, you dislike your job. Is the issue the work or your manager? If you had a different manager, would you enjoy your work more? If being underpaid is the driving force behind you disliking your job, are there other companies that you could move to that would pay you more? If you could work from home a couple of days a week, would you be happier?

What I'm getting at here is the root issue. While you may think a different line of work would make you happy, the real problem could be your manager or your company's policies. If you are going to take a drastic step like switching to an entirely different industry or line of work, or even going to grad school, it's important to know exactly what it is you are expecting to be different.

Let's say you are an accountant and you realize that what you enjoy is work that is more creative and has fewer boundaries and rules. In this case it very well could make sense to pivot to a different line of work that plays more to your strengths. You may have to take a lower-paying job to make the career change work, so it's important to be sure taking a new job truly will be the positive change you think it will be. There's always the possibility the change in careers will end up being "just another job" you dislike.

Leverage Your Time Outside of Work

Even if you know you won't be working in your current job or career long-term, there may be benefits to staying for the short term or even the foreseeable future. What I've seen in the past five or so years is that most people are looking to be self-employed business owners. Less common is someone looking to, say, move from one line of work at an employer to another line of work at another employer. What they ultimately want is flexibility and control over where, when, and how they work. If this is the underlying desire, whether someone is willing to admit it or not, simply switching to a different type of job won't make them happy.

If you fall into this group, I highly recommend you leverage your time outside of work. What I mean by that is, start doing what you want to be doing while you are still gainfully employed. We live in a world where so much can be done outside of your nine-to-five to help lay the foundation of a business or self-employment setup. It's a good test of "how bad do you want it" as well. If working for yourself is going to work out for you, you should be willing to sacrifice a decent amount of your free time to set yourself up for success. Depending on what you are trying to do, it can even be possible to build your business to a full-time income level before you quit your day job (in fact, this is the ideal and recommended scenario).

Kelsey Fecho, a freelance full-stack web developer, started her career in corporate finance. While she was working in finance, she kept coding on the side. Eventually she had enough freelance experience and clients to make the switch. She recommends working on the side first before leaving your nine-to-five. "It definitely helps to try out your new field as a side-hustle. Not only will making a little extra money help free yourself, but you also gain experience and contacts to help propel your career forward in whatever new direction you decide."

If you aren't looking to work for yourself, this advice is still relevant. For example, if you are interested in marketing but have no degree or experience in it, learn as much as you can about it and gain any experience you can outside of your nine-to-five. You can then leverage that knowledge and experience to make you an easy hire when you start applying to marketing jobs.

There is much more that can be said about how student loans impact careers, the work we do, and entrepreneurship. At the very least, I hope this book has given you some helpful advice on how to organize and feel in control of your student loans and financial life, as well as what specific actions you can take to set yourself up for success later on.

You've got big things ahead of you, and it would be a shame if you let student loans get in the way. You can do this!

Key Takeaways

- Student loans have been shown to correlate to poorer psychological functioning. Be aware of how they are impacting your mental health.

- If you are experiencing stress, anxiety, or depression from student loans (or otherwise), seek out a counselor or therapist.

- Be open and honest about your financial situation with your partner. Expect respect from them.

- Paying for a wedding while repaying student loan debt is possible. Use a wedding budget and make it a challenge to find opportunities to save money.

- Prioritize your wedding budget. Drastically cut costs on the things you don't care about so that you can put money toward the things you do care about.

- If you hate the career field that you went to school for, give yourself permission to leave for a career you enjoy.

- If you are making a career pivot, create and work through an exit plan that includes building an emergency fund, gaining relevant skills, and learning as much as you can about your new career field before making the leap.

Acknowledgments

I would first like to thank anyone and everyone who has supported me in my pursuit of helping people improve their financial lives. I would not have had the opportunity to write this important book if it wasn't for you. It's been quite the journey and I am so grateful for anyone who has read and shared my content over the past seven years.

I want to thank everyone at Mango who helped make this book possible, especially my editor Hugo Villabona, as well as Chris McKenney, Hannah Paulsen, Michele Jessica Fievre, Roberto Núñez and Robin Miller.

Thank you to Marla Urban, who meticulously reviewed multiple copies of the manuscript. Her comments, questions, and edits truly made this book the best it could be.

A big thanks to Rachel Slifka, who took on an increased workload for *Young Adult Money* while I researched and wrote the book.

Thank you to anyone who has shared encouraging words; they do not go unnoticed.

And finally, thank you to my wife, Victoria, who has not once wavered in supporting me as I pursued my dreams. She has sacrificed greatly as I've worked a nine-to-five job while pouring countless hours into my projects. This book would not have happened without you.

Resources and References

Federal Student Aid

https://studentaid.ed.gov

This is the official website for Federal Student Aid, which is an office within the Department of Education. The website is packed with a ton of information on student loans, including many of the topics covered in this book that may be relevant to your situation (forbearance, deferment, income-driven repayment plans, etc.).

StudentLoans.gov

https://studentloans.gov/

This is another website run by the Office of Federal Student Aid. The most important feature on this site is the repayment estimator. It's also where you will go to apply for loan consolidation as well as to apply for and submit annual recertification for an IDR plan.

National Student Loan Data System

https://www.nslds.ed.gov/npas/index.htm

This is where you can find information on all your federal student loans, such as what types of loans you have, how much is left to repay on each loan, and more.

Having Issues with a Loan Servicer? You Can File Complaints at the Following:

Submit a Complaint with the Department of Education: https://feedback.studentaid.ed.gov/

Submit a Complaint with the Consumer Financial Protection Bureau: https://www.consumerfinance.gov/complaint/

About the Author

David Carlson is a nationally recognized millennial personal finance author and speaker. He is the author of *Hustle Away Debt*, which is focused on helping people pay down their debt faster through side hustles. He is the founder of YoungAdultMoney.com, a website focused on helping those in their twenties and thirties make more, save more, and live better. His opinions have been featured in media outlets including *The Washington Post*, *The New York Times*, NBC's KARE 11, Cheddar, and YAHOO! Finance. He lives in Minneapolis with his wife Victoria and their two very spoiled cats.